C   r RN

to his   Scapa Flow

with   urier RN

Edited by Harriet Bachrach

FOREWORD by MAJOR GENERAL JULIAN THOMPSON CB OBE

HMS *Calliope* (*National Maritime Museum*) Commodore Le Mesurier's flag ship of the 4th Light Cruiser Squadron at Jutland. 'Calliope' (pronounced Cal-eye-oh-pe) was the mother of Orpheus, the ancient Greek poet and musician who ventured into Hades to rescue his wife, Eurydice. HMS *Calliope* weighed 3,750 tons, measured 420ft x 41.5ft x 14.75ft (128m x 12.6m x 4.5m), had 2 six-inch (150mm), 8 four-inch (200mm) guns, 2 torpedo tubes (21in) mounted above the waterline, a top speed of 29.5 knots and a complement of 324 men. Her displacement ranged from 4228 tons to 4695 tons with a deep load. She was launched from Chatham Dockyard on 17 December 1914. In this new class of ship the boilers were rearranged and the number of funnels reduced from four to two, beginning the classic C class cruiser profile. *Calliope*'s armour belt was thin: 4in–1.5in (100mm–40mm), deck 1in (25mm) and CT 6in (150mm). Le Mesurier fought against heavier plating as 'the speed of these little ships is their chief safeguard'. In 1918 *Calliope*'s length overall increased to 446 ft (135.9 m) with the addition of High Speed Sweeps fitted and a 'flying-off' platform forward. All the ships in the 4th LCS at Jutland: *Calliope, Constance, Caroline, Royalist* and *Comus* survived the Great War.

Cover background: British Grand Fleet at Jutland 1916 *(Robert Hunt Library)*

First published in the United Kingdom in 2006 by
Wessex Books, 2 Station Cottages, Newton Toney, Salisbury, Wilts SP4 0HD.
Tel/Fax: 01980 629349   www.wessexbooks.co.uk   E-mail: info@wessexbooks.co.uk
Text © Harriet Bachrach 2006
Design and layout © Wessex Books 2006
Cover design by Alexander S. Grenfell
Printed in Great Britain by Short-Run Press
ISBN 1-903035-26-0

Contents

In most cases I have kept to my grandfather's original spellings and punctuation, but I have altered them if there is a possibility of ambiguity.

Harriet Bachrach
December 2005

The Royal Navy continued to give its young officers and sailors their seamanship training under sail until 1903, and HMS *Cruiser* was one of the last two ships to do this. Charles Le Mesurier had spent four months in a similar ship in 1887 as part of his training. In 1914 ships looked very different.

H.M.S CALLIOPE

Foreword to
Commodore Charles Le Mesurier's Letters

Julian Thompson

Commodore Charles Le Mesurier who commanded the 4th Light Cruiser Squadron in the Grand Fleet at Jutland was one of the few senior Royal Navy officers who used their initiative in that battle. But he was far too modest to say so, even when unburdening himself to his wife in letters written after Jutland and published here by his granddaughter, Harriet Bachrach.

Le Mesurier's 4th Light Cruiser Squadron at Jutland consisted of the *Calliope* (wearing his Broad Pennant), *Constance*, *Caroline*, *Royalist*, and *Comus*. These were modern (laid down in 1914 or later), fast 28-29 knot, potent ships, with, depending on their class, two or four shaft turbines, oil-fired boilers, two 6-inch and six or eight 4-inch guns, as well as two or four 21-inch torpedo tubes. Professor Marder in his brilliant five-volume work *From the Dreadnought to Scapa Flow: The Royal Navy in the Fisher Era, 1904–1919*, misjudges Commodore Le Mesurier's ability, labelling him 'average'. This is at odds with Le Mesurier's record at Jutland, and that of his cruiser squadron, which must be rated as considerably above average.

The clue to his approach to war, and training for war, lies in a remark made in one of his letters to his wife, where he says; 'you must leave things to individual initiative in these very high speed little ships – there is no time to make signals – I am very pleased with the way my few 'Action' signals were taken in and acted on'. Le Mesurier appears to have practised what we now call 'Mission Command', in other words he told his captains what he wanted done, but not how to do it; the very opposite of the principles underlying Admiral Sir John Jellicoe's voluminous Grand Fleet Battle Orders (GFBOs). These attempted to list every conceivable action that the enemy might take, and provide a correct response, every single one of which would be initiated by the appropriate signal to be found in GFBOs. Unfortunately, by 1914, over 100 years had elapsed since the Royal Navy had fought a fleet action against a first class enemy. Most officers lacked experience of battle, and being schooled in a rigid Victorian system that emphasised obedience, were inclined to await orders from their seniors before taking action. They were unprepared for the uncertainties of warfighting where the battle-wise practitioner is not dismayed if having assessed that the enemy has only four courses of action open to him, he chooses the fifth. Put another way, the enemy thinks too, and may opt for the unexpected, which is almost invariably not catered for.

Jellicoe, or 'JRJ' in the letters, was not a 'mission command' man, although Le Mesurier in company with many in the Grand Fleet held 'JRJ' in great regard; and the 4th Light Cruiser Squadron was nicknamed 'John Jellicoe's Own'. But the outcome of the Battle of Jutland might have been different if Jellicoe heading south-east with his battlefleet to meet Beatty coming north-west with the Battle Cruiser Fleet (BCF), had stationed 'John Jellicoe's Own' correctly. He kept Le Mesurier's light cruisers on a tight rein just ahead of his battle squadron columns. Had Jellicoe deployed them in their proper role of scouting well ahead, he might have established contact with Beatty earlier, and not had to signal him to ask 'where is the enemy battlefleet?' as Beatty's flagship, *Lion*, emerged from the swirling mist and gun smoke pursued by the said battlefleet, still not visible astern of the BCF. Beatty failed to keep his master fully in the picture. But had Jellicoe's 'own' cruisers been in a position to provide him with the position, course and speed of the enemy, he might have completed the Grand Fleet's deployment into line of battle, by the time Scheer's battlefleet emerged from the murk. Instead he was still swinging his battle squadrons into position. Only Jellicoe's quick thinking and making the right decision to deploy on the port wing column, prevented Scheer from catching the Grand Fleet still in cruising array, or deploying on the starboard wing column; either could have spelt disaster.

Later, in the last daylight actions, Scheer in desperation launched his destroyers at the Grand Fleet. Le Mesurier's captains were the only ones to use their initiative and, accompanied by destroyers, attacked the attackers, breaking through the enemy destroyer screen to sight three battleships, *Prinzregent Luitpold*, *Kaiser* and *Markgraf*. The British destroyers fled from these tempting targets, but *Calliope* pressed on, and fired a torpedo at the battleships. She was then hit, putting two guns out of action, killing ten men and wounding twenty-three.

Just before daylight faded, *Calliope*, *Caroline* and *Royalist* of 4th Light Cruiser Squadron sighting the battleships *Westfalen* and *Nassau* at the head of Scheer's line, and again using their initiative, swung in to attack only to be ordered to haul off by 2nd Battle Squadron's commander, Vice-Admiral Sir Martyn Jerram, but not before they had fired one torpedo each. Had Jerram followed up, he might have crushed the head of Scheer's line, forced him to head west, and ultimately prevented his escape.

The letters give us much more than a description of these incidents. They provide vivid insights into the social history of the First World War Royal Navy through the eyes of one of its senior commanders, as well as affectionate asides to his wife Florence ('Foffs') whom he clearly adored. The snippets of family gossip are all the more tantalizing for being one-sided; unfortunately Florence's letters no longer exist.

He was a very modern man, caring for his sailors, and writing to widows or parents of men killed in action, and asking 'Foffs' to do likewise, as well as following up the progress of the wounded. He was inclined to be a radical, and the antithesis of a bluff old sea dog still clinging to Victorian ways,

Commodore C.E. Le Mesurier RN (1869–1917) as a Captain.

Died of Wounds
_____

✓ William Collins Pti   Father   Mr Benjamin Collins
                                    36 Alvey Street
                                    Walworth. S.E.

✓ Thomas Trish A.B.   Father   Mr William Trish
                                    8 Star Cottages
                                    Chipstead, Redhill
                                                Surrey

✓ Sidney Elliss A.B.   Mother   Mrs Elliss
                                    7 Hardwicke Street
                                    Barking. Essex

Severely Wounded
(on Fore Bridge)

Halcraw Leadg Signalman   Wife   Mrs Halcraw
                                    58 Meary Street
                                    South Shields

Walker Boy 1st Class (Bugler) Mother Mrs Walker
                                    21 Hunstore Road
                                    Kennington Cross
                                        London S.E.

A page from the enclosures of Letter 4 showing the name of 'Boy' (Bill) Walker among the list of the Severely Wounded (on Fore Bridge).

4

commonplace among many of his peers. He articulates this view in one letter, 'Funny what a hide-bound set we are – never will de-centralise'.

'The Sunday rags absolutely beneath contempt', wrote Le Mesurier, and again, 'I have mislaid my copy of the Morning Liar'. His views on the press will strike a chord with officers today who view many media folk with distaste for their readiness to whinge, denigrate the efforts of the armed services, and embellish stories to the point of downright lying. Le Mesurier quotes one journalist criticising the pronouncements of another's piece in a rival paper, as 'not only arm-chair strategy, but grandmother in the arm-chair strategy'.

Politicians get a broadside, 'If a fellow in Government service makes a mistake, down he goes, but a Cabinet Minister can be as incompetent or lazy as he pleases, and nothing happens'; this still resonates today, although one might add to Le Mesurier's list of ministerial shortcomings: telling lies, and using one's position for one's own benefit or that of a friend or mistress — nothing changes.

The 'service' gossip is lively, and includes Le Mesurier's opinion that the 'sailor son in *Collingwood* looks twice the man his elder brother of Wales is'; comparing the sub-lieutenant in the battleship *Collingwood*'s A Turret, who was to become George VI following the abdication of his elder sibling Edward VIII. Le Mesurier never lived to see his opinion, which many would share, validated, because he died of cancer in November 1917, having relinquished command to go sick in July that year. Thus he never gained the promotion to Rear Admiral that he so richly deserved, the prospects of which he frequently mentioned in his letters to 'Foffs'. Harriet Bachrach has done us all a service by publishing these letters, now deposited in the Archives of the Department of Documents in the Imperial War Museum in London.

Florence 'Foffs' Le Mesurier (1874–1946) in 1912.

5

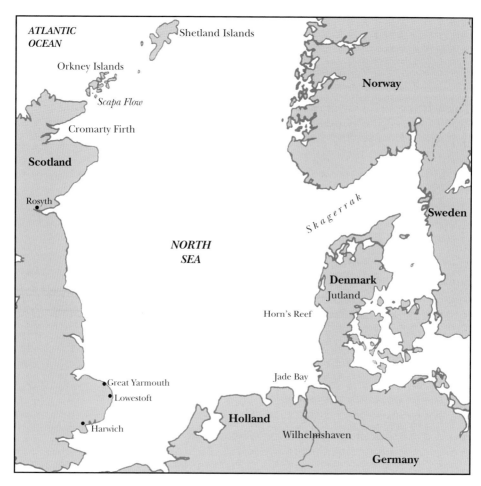

The Battle of Jutland (May 31, 1916), known to Germans as the Battle of the Skagerrak, was hailed
by them as a victory. British losses were higher: 14 ships and 6,097 lives compared with the
Germans' 11 ships and 2,551 lives. But afterwards the Germans stayed in harbour while the British
retained control of the North Sea. Then the Germans increased their use of submarines.

Every sailor's pet dream: The Grand Fleet at sea. This impressive picture, taken in good light on
calm waters does not reveal problems that could arise in fog, wind or darkness. At Jutland the
Grand Fleet was outlined against the sunset so could be seen by the enemy, while British ships
were blinded by smoke blown towards them from the High Seas Fleet. As evening drew in on
Wednesday May 31 it was hard to read signals or find targets. *(Imperial War Museum Q22883)*

Introduction

By Harriet Bachrach

These letters are a significant eye-witness record of the famous battle and its aftermath made by a senior participant. A terrifying picture emerges of a navy and society struggling to enter a fast-changing world of new technology, a dark world with little social policy and awash with appalling new tricks of war. It is history in the making, and offers new insights to the puzzle of a battle that even in its 90th anniversary still needs answers.

Personal letters are fast becoming things of the past as mobile phones, text messages and emails take over. Back in 1916 no such options existed. From June 2 to October 3, 1916 my grandfather, Commodore Charles E. Le Mesurier RN, commander of HMS *Calliope* and the 4th Light Cruiser Squadron, wrote 76 letters and three postcards to his wife Florence ('Foffs') from the Grand Fleet. There are also three letters to his teenage son Ted (E.K. Le Mesurier) a future captain of HMS *Belfast*. Some thirty 'last' letters home from the Grand Fleet as he prepared to go on sick leave in 1917 and from Guy's Hospital near London Bridge complete the score. These have been more heavily edited than the ones immediately following the famous battle, which, dashed off from the scene of action are a primary, substantially untapped historical source. Short extracts appeared in *The Naval Review* in October 1999, *The Orcadian* newspaper (January 2000) and in Julian Thompson's recent (2005) book, *The Imperial War Museum Book of the War at Sea 1914–1918*. I am most grateful to Major General Thompson for his authoritative Foreword showing a wealth of historical knowledge, personal military experience and his archivist's insight into 'the words of the men who fought'.

It is hard for us today to realise how long it took for messages to get through in 1916. Jutland is a prime example, from the bungled information about the whereabouts of the High Seas Fleet on May 31, to the lack of contact between battle divisions of the Grand Fleet and the curse of signals misread or unseen.

Poor Foffs was kept in the dark too. Telephones and 'wires' were for military use or to notify deaths, and on June 2 Charles chose to signal his continued existence with a postcard. His letter of June 10 shows how aware he was of his wife's anguish: 'I found your letter of 6th waiting and rejoiced to think your suspense was over; next time I will send a harmless wire.'

She may have shuddered at the words 'next time' but was probably not fooled by her husband's first words: 'All serene and very jolly', intended no doubt for the censor, usually the ship's doctor or chaplain. These men would have had their hands full after Jutland and Le Mesurier got away with a lot, especially as he sometimes censored his letters himself, as he did while waiting for his 'new ugly duckling' (HMS *Cambrian*) to join the 4th Light Cruiser Squadron later in 1916.

He was always waiting 'to let 'em have it properly next time', looking at Jutland as a good 'dress rehearsal'. But after the battle the Germans opted for submarine and mine tactics instead of risking their High Seas Fleet in open combat. My grandfather's opinion, 'They got as much as they had stomach for and were badly rattled' seems spot-on, as does his assessment of the near-engagement of the two fleets on the weekend of August 18/19, 1916: ''Tis rather 'Puss-in-the-Corner': if we go over to pay them a visit we have to look out for their torpedo craft.'

After Jutland the Grand Fleet was ready within days for 'another smack at 'em'. No wonder, then, that Le Mesurier ignored the onset of the cancer of the oesophagus that killed him in 1917 – he probably thought he had only a touch of indigestion. He smoked a pipe, worked day and night, took little home leave and existed on 'slops' (slang for naval stores) and SECURITY!' (Letter from Guy's, October 5, 1917). Medical inspections happened during recruitment and officers 'can't afford to go sick in war time'. Perhaps he pulled rank to evade medical check-ups; perhaps they were not obligatory. With hindsight readers can spot the signs: forgetting to thank his indignant wife for the gift of a fruit cake and needing to 'walk off' a heavy lunch.

His wife did not guess his true condition until he came home on leave in the summer of 1917. During their 17 years of married life they were nearly always apart. Charles served in HMS *Hannibal* (Channel Fleet) 1900–5, *Hindustan* (Atlantic and Channel Fleets 1905–8) and then, after his promotion to Captain in June 1908, in the RN War College where, after a time in HMS *Theseus* (a twin screw Protected Cruiser) he became Flag Captain under the Vice Admiralship of the Hon Sir Alexander E Bethell in January 1913.

They had four children: Ted in December 1903 and Margaret in 1905. The home posting resulted in the births of the two 'big babies', my mother

Alice (1909–86) and her sister Anne (1910–52), within 16 months of each other. The two girls always competed for their mother's attention but there was never enough to go round. The eldest daughter Margaret (1905–74) had residual polio so Foffs was fully occupied. Their father showed his understanding of this in a sympathetic letter to his son Ted, when she failed to buy him a birthday present. Today we know how much the healthy siblings suffer in a family where another's needs predominate but I imagine it was unusual to think like this then.

Alice Le Mesurier (the editor's mother).

Anne Le Mesurier.

Studio portrait of Margaret ('My Mouse')
and Ted ('the small son').

The Le Mesuriers hailed originally from the Channel Islands and most of them left to find greater scope abroad. This may explain Charles Le Mesurier's 'radical' thinking, noted by Major General Thompson in his perceptive Foreword. It was an irony of Fate that they exchanged one small community for another: the minuscule island of Alderney for the tiny ex-patriate 'colony' around Genoa. No wonder then that Charles chose the navy, or that the love-smitten Foffs accepted her charming young sailor and a wider life in England.

The couple did some of their courting at Portofino, where Foffs's uncle Monty Yeats Brown had restored a castle. His son, Francis Yeats Brown, wrote *The Bengal Lancer*, a best selling novel about India showing respect for and knowledge of Indian life. My father, Douglas Carter, a civil servant who met Alice through his friendship with her sister Anne at Cambridge University, used to recall Foffs closing the curtains when her scantily-clad cousin Francis, an early yoga buff, did his practice in her garden at Emsworth on the south coast. The Letters at that time reposed safely in her possession there.

These family papers and photographs came with Margaret , ('my Mouse' in the Letters), when she moved to Sutton, Surrey, to live with my family after her mother and younger sister died. It was a complicated move. My mother Alice, Charles and Foffs's third child, had just started full-time work after the youngest of her four children began school and the new house had to be adapted to Margaret's needs. The letters were chucked in an attic where they remained out of sight and mind for nearly 50 years, when my brother Michael and I cleared out my parents' last house in 1998.

There were also letters from Charles's father, Edward 'Algy' Le Mesurier dating from February 2, 1880 when his wife died. He wrote to his widowed elder sister Agnes Gretton in Australia asking her to come and look after his 'orphans'. These letters yielded much family background: Foffs was five years younger than Charles, hence his frequent endearment, 'my child'. Their families supported each other in times of joy and grief.

Sign of the times – new bicycles. The Le Mesurier girls ride their new bicycles – a great novelty – under the watchful eye of their Aunt Agnes Gretton, in a wheelchair pulled by a sturdy servant.

Foffs was bridesmaid to Charles's sister Margaret in 1896 at her marriage to Arnold Inman. The couple soon produced Nell-Nell (b.1897) whose gift of books to the sailors was 'much appreciated' – Were these words also a coded message – that the sick bay was full on June 2, 1916?

Families were impossibly large. Charles's mother, Elizabeth (née Wilson) Le Mesurier had seven children in 13 years, Foffs's mother, Alice (née Yeats-Brown) Kirby five in 11, losing a child in infancy. When Charles's mother died at the age of 38 in February 1880, Alice Kirby visited the stricken widower to let him talk about his loss. 'Algy' Le Mesurier worked with Foffs's father Harry Kirby in the Granet & Brown Bank in Genoa (later requisitioned by Mussolini; Monty Yeats Brown wisely forestalled a similar fate by presenting the Italian state with his castle at Portofino).

Their common background, interests and values gave the Commodore and his wife a close knowledge of each other's minds. To clarify meanings without upsetting the censor became a sort of game. He often alluded to novels they both knew such as Owen Wister's *The Virginian*, Thackeray's *The Newcomes* and H.G. Wells's *Love and Mr Lewisham*. A copy of *The Virginian* (1907 edition) was in the attic too, strapped up with the black sticky-back plastic that preceded cellotape.

The couple's concern for the welfare of junior officers, widows and the wounded bore fruit. It is good to know that the 15-year-old bugler, 'Boy Walker' survived having a shell splinter removed from his chest and received the gift of an inscribed bugle from King George V for his 'gallantry' at Jutland.

Charles and Foffs knew what it meant to care for an invalid. Margaret contracted polio during the hot summer of 1911 after visiting Portsmouth, where the town authorities failed to issue warnings for fear of scaring away the summer visitors. One of her legs stopped growing when she was six, the other at age 11. Her parents tried alternative medicine, 'Swedish water treatment' in Highgate, north London and it must have helped as my aunt was nearly 70 when she died of heart failure in a Streatham nursing home on the day her

The Kirby children *c*.1888–9. Willie (seated), Hetty, Lizzie and 'Foffs'.

11

C.E. Le Mesurier as a young cadet, *c*.1884. He was promoted to Commodore 2nd class on 15 May 1915 in charge of the 4th Light Cruiser Squadron.

cousin Dr Mary (Medge) Egerton made a chance visit. Medge was the daughter of Charles's sister Lou, and his talkative brother-in-law Willie, who billeted themselves on Foffs in 1916 when they and their three children were on home leave from the Indian Civil Service. That last unscheduled Egerton visit surely cancelled any remaining debt.

The entire collection is of value to military, social, family and political historians. Time 'fast-forwarded' in the Commodore's life, from the heyday of empire to the hell of the trenches, from undisputed mastery of the seas to near disaster as German mines and submarines starved Britain of food and raw materials in early 1917. Only the success of the convoy system prevented this. Le Mesurier went from cadetship in 1882 in the hulk of HMS *Britannia* (later abandoned for health reasons) to ships powered successively by wind, steam, coal and oil to the highly technical twin-turbined light cruiser he commanded at Jutland.

Another huge change looms. How many grandchildren of today's military heroes and heroines will discover such a 'cache' in the attic? Private letters are dying out. Such verbal snapshots are rare now. My grandfather may make mistakes in his instant reportage, and occasionally expose his ignorance, as when he misjudged the fast promotion of the 33-year-old genius Lt Cdr Martin Nasmith (later Adm Sir), the submariner who invented the ISWAS range-finding system. But his letters to his wife give a truer picture and record of the time and how people experienced it than any official report or private journal could begin to achieve.

The gap between executive 'command' officers and their technical staff – engineers and other specialists – was wide, dangerous and riddled with snobbery. The Commodore's son, Captain E.K. Le Mesurier, comments on this in his thought-provoking Recollections at the end of the book, written shortly before he died. This gap could be seen at Jutland.

Letters sent from HMS *Calliope*

1. *Postcard, Friday 2 June 1916*

All serene and very jolly. Have put everyone on a regime of p.c.'s for a couple of days. So can only send you scraps. Your last – 26th. All will yet go well with Atta.[1] Please let Nell-Nell[2] know her books much appreciated.

C

2. *Postcard, Saturday 3 June 1916*

All goes well and feel much more cheery after a good night in – your last letter 31st – glad the Admiralty has published all details: Don't credit *ALL* you read in the German W/T press message?! Tell the Mouse I am sending her a 'souvenir'.[3]

Yr:

C

1. Harriet Kirby, Mrs Le Mesurier's sister.
2. Charles Le Mesurier's niece Nell Inman.
3. 'The Mouse' was Charles Le Mesurier's nickname for his daughter Margaret. The 'souvenir' was a piece of shrapnel.

Hetty Kirby ('Atta'), Foffs's sister and an artist.

3. *Sunday 4 June 1916*

Well, Sweetheart: Where shall I begin? And how much will the good censor let pass? I think my first impression is one of thankfulness. We were in a tight place – Look up our beloved *The Virginian*.[1] When the author is driven by the Virginian from the Railway station to the Judge's ranch – and the horses in the buggy bolt going down hill. *The Virginian* says 'I reckon you're half-way between "Well I'm ——" and "Thank God"——'.

'Twas a misty evening: the Battle cruisers and the four *Barhams* – were coming across to meet us, of the main body, at a meeting place, when the light cruisers ahead of David Beatty crashed into them – the German battle cruisers ahead, with the whole High Sea Fleet behind. After a certain amount of preliminary scrapping, the action settled down into a fight between the 5 German Battle-cruisers and our six – with the four *Barhams* (5th Battle Squadron), somewhat in rear engaging the High Sea Fleet – our main body coming up. Result – a good deal in favour of the Germans. When the High Sea Fleet realised they were running bang into Jellicoe, they naturally turned so that practically only their rear – original leading-divisions, were brought to action. We were mixed up at the head of our battle fleet line in a first class scrimmage as the Battle cruiser action passed across our front: we then got sorted out a bit, and got our five little ships in correct station.

Our first chance came about 7.30 o/c. when they slipped some destroyers at our leading battle squadron: got two of the German T.B.D's [torpedo boat destroyers] on that occasion. And luckily all their torpedoes missed us. (Four close to *Calliope*) – Our second little excursion came soon after 8 o/c: another German destroyer attack: This time I only took out three ships: we pushed the German destroyers back, when suddenly, out of the haze, loomed large the High Sea Fleet about 4 miles off: we held on a bit and fired torpedos at 'em – *CALLIOPE* has good ground for thinking that hers got home[2] – and then ran like billy-oh for shelter – with at least three big battle-ships plunking at us. A most uncomfortable five or ten minutes, as their shooting was 100 A1 – we were hit, in *Calliope*, three times, and lost, I am sorry to say, close on a dozen killed, with many wounded. Another little scrap, quite a mild one, about 9 o/c – and then peace at our end of the line – tho' 'twas a key actions night. – Next morning we swept back for cripples: our destroyers bagged a big'un 'bout 2 a.m. – and so home. A somewhat unsatisfactory meeting: we have NOT put 'em off the board tho' the losses about work out equal -I am afraid Maurice Bethell has gone. Our other friends, Cay[3] and so on – you know already – for I am very glad that the Admiralty had the sound sense to own up. And so, my dear, you must not lose heart. We have our main fleet intact while theirs is distinctly weakened. The main situation has not changed, tho' this meeting will quite naturally put heart into the Germans: and a deuced good fight they put up – tho' they got badly rattled – I have your letters of 26th, 30th and 31st.

I only hope you were not too anxious until you got my post card? 'Tis good to realise Atta is really better. Hard work that nursing: I went over to the hospital ship yesterday evening, with No 1 to look at the wounded and could get an idea of what hard work it is when a rush comes. They are cheery fellows, the British blue – and incomprehensible! Their principal anxiety, as expressed to me, when I saw them, was whether they would get compensation for the clothes cut off them when they were bowled over!

Heart up, my dear. Hug the chicks

Yr: C

1. *The Virginian* by the American author, Owen Wister, was published in July 1902, and went into 15 editions before the Le M's 1907 edition published by Macmillan with illustrations by Arthur I. Keller. The passage referred to is on pp 54–55. 'Help was too far away to do anything for us. We passed scathless through a part of the cattle: I saw their horns and backs go by. Some earth crumbled, and we plunged downward into water, rocking among stones, and upward again through some more crumbling earth . . . A dry gully was coming and no room to turn. The farther side of it was terraced with rock. We should simply fall backward, if we did not fall forward first. He steered the horses straight over, and just at the bottom swung them, with astonishing skill, to the right along the hard-baked mud . . .

   I looked at the trustworthy man, and smiled vaguely. He considered me for a moment.

   'I reckon,' said he, 'you're feelin' about half-way between "Oh, Lord!" and "Thank God!"'

   'That's quite it,' said I, as he got down on the ground.

   'Nothing's broke,' said he, after a searching examination. And he indulged in a true Victorian expletive. 'Gentlemen, hush!' he murmured gently, looking at me with his grave eyes; 'one time I got pretty near scared. You, Buck,' he continued, 'some folks would beat you now till yu'd be uncertain whether you was a hawss or a railway accident . . .'

2. It did not. The torpedoes then in use were only effective if they hit dead-on. The casings were too thick and used up much ammunition on impact, or bounced off instead of penetrating their targets.

3. Captain A.L Cay commanded HMS *Invincible,* 3rd Battlecruiser Squadron.

4. *Tuesday 6 June 1916*

Sweetheart. That's a very plucky letter of yours of the 3rd when you had seen the papers: a very plucky letter and I am very proud of you. Really our Press gives me the fantals:[1] The all Tory papers *Times, Globe, Morning Post* went off at half cock with Jeremiahs of the deepest purple: Damned if I don't turn Radical. I am more than inclined to, and have been for some years – The *Westminster Gazette* was quite sound, *Daily Chronicle* stupidly rabid.

Sunday rags absolutely beneath contempt – yelling for Jacky[2] to come back – and for every VAL's head, in command at sea, to be cut off! Makes me sick. The truth, my child, is that we missed the chance of annihilating Germany at sea: on the other hand, they got as much as they had any stomach for, and were badly rattled. While + and – about balance. Let us keep our heads – NOT despise our enemy – as we were rather prone to do – and make up our minds to let 'em have it properly next time – that's all I am going to say now.

Just like old Giffard[3:] a selfish old man, too tired to come into Southsea so rings you up – knowing full well your own anxieties and troubles and pushes his own dirty work on to you – Damn his eyes – I am sending you, my Heart, a list of our poor fellows who have gone or who are dangerously wounded: I have written myself to each, with one exception – duly marked – WO. I will write as well, so all will have had my own letter. I want you to write a line as well? Particularly to the Sergeant of Marine's widow. And to the mother of Hogan, my steward. Tell 'em all you have heard from me how well *Calliope*'s behaved. You can also write to Mrs Tate and give her a *cautious* summary of what I have told you, but be wary for the old boy has a tongue of the loosest description, and your Charles E. doesn't want to be mixed up in the bickering that must almost inevitably take place. Write Lady Bethell too: I wrote the old man on Sunday – Heart up, my child. All goes well with the State.

Yr: C

1. Give (a person) the fantals, make him restless, uneasy. *The Penguin Dictionary of Historical Slang*.
2. Admiral Sir John Fisher was First Sea Lord in 1914 but resigned in 1915 over the Dardanelles campaign.
3. George A. Giffard had been C.E. Le M's Captain in HMS *Hannibal* 1902–03.

Enclosed: [1, 2]

Died of Wounds

William COLLINS <u>Pte</u>	<u>Father</u>	Mr BENJAMIN COLLINS 36 ALVEY STREET WALWORTH. S.E.
Thomas TRISH A.B.	<u>Father</u>	Mr WILLIAM TRISH 8 STAR COTTAGES

		CHIPSTEAD, REDHILL SURREY
Sidney ELLISS A.B.	Mother	Mrs ELLISS 7 HARDWICKE STREET BARKING. ESSEX

Severely Wounded
(on FORE BRIDGE)

HALCROW Leading Signalman	Wife	Mrs HALCROW 50 IMEARY STREET SOUTH SHIELDS
WALKER Boy 1st class (Bugler)	Mother	Mrs WALKER 21 HUNSTORE ROAD KENNINGTON CROSS LONDON S.E.

Killed

Sergeant A.W. BALCOMBE R.M.L.I.	Wife	Mrs BALCOMBE 13 REFORM ROAD LUTON CHATHAM
Walter FAIRWEATHER A.B.	Mother	Mrs FAIRWEATHER 16 RECTORY ROAD ORFORD SUFFOLK
Joseph SKIDMORE Stoker	Mother	Mrs SKIDMORE 36 CHAPMAN STREET WEST BROMWICH STAFFS
Thomas HOGAN Commodore's steward	Mother	Mrs HOGAN 7 GREEN WOOD TERRACE BOUNDARY LANE EVERTON LIVERPOOL
William ROWLINGSON A.B.	Mother	Mrs ROWLINGSON GREAT WRATTING Nr HAVERHILL SUFFOLK
Frederick HORSFALL Private	Sister	Mrs SPIERS 33 BARGE HOUSE ROAD NORTH WOOLWICH S.E.
Thomas SUTCLIFFE Stoker	Mother	Mrs SUTCLIFFE 11 GEORGE STREET GRAys,[3] ESSEX

1. In the original, each name has been ticked in pencil, presumably by Mrs Le M.
2. Ten out of the 12 next of kin are women, seven mothers, two wives, one sister, and two fathers.
3. The discrepancy in capital letters in 'GRAys' may indicate the writer's fatigue.

5. *Wednesday 7 June 1916*

Sweetheart. Yrs: of Sunday: that day I was still rather edgy: we had our own Memorial service here – and then toddled off on shore to attend the big 'un. I had a first class serious heart to heart talk with one of my fellows – and probably wanted more sleep! All serene now and I am tame enough to feed out of anybody's hand!

While the holes in our transom are being fast covered up – C-in-C sent for me this morning, to talk shop, and told me with a twinkle in his eye that 'the various reports are coming in fast now, and the number of explosions seen, or heard, after firing torpedoes, is prodigious'! A sly dig at me, 'cos I maintain stoutly that ours got home!

One of our destroyers fetched safely into harbour on the East coast with sixty feet of plating ex: a German light cruiser sticking to her bows! –

That was a bad smash – poor Savill in *Hampshire*[1] and very rough on K. of K: they had all been on board the Fleet flagship that very day, leaving at tea-time. Blowing hard, as luck had it. Lemme see – News? – Nothing doing up here: I am longing to get to sea again, stopping in harbour is very bad for one: two of my little ships had 20 hours in harbour, after we got back t'other day, and were pushed out for three days patrol, and are all the better for it! . . . Glad to see the newspapers are taking a saner view of things naval, but 'twill take some time to get rid of the unpleasant impression left on one after reading Saturday and Sunday last.   Night-night   Yr: C

1. HMS *Hampshire* struck a mine off Marwick Head, Orkney, on June 5, with Lord Kitchener on board.

6. *Friday 9 June 1916*

Sweetheart: All serene and better weather. I have yours of 5th, a Monday, and had hoped you would have got my first p.c. that morning? We got in here 'bout 11.30 on the Friday of that week and started to transfer our serious cases as soon as we anchored – but I didn't get into my cabins until early afternoon, as Martin and his brigade had naturally a good deal of tidying up to do after the cots had been taken out. BUT – I wrote you a p.c. in time to catch the evening's mail. I must look into it – C-in-C sent for me 3 o/c and then I had to interview my own Captains, but eventually tumbled into bed at 8.30 and slept 'werry 'eavy'.

Here is the boy's letter: I have marked, with blue pencil, what was the result of rank stupidity at the Admiralty – I see Balfour[1] blames the Press for writing such unwarrantably pessimistic leading articles? How can he excuse the form of the first communiqué? – And, what is much worse – how can he justify having allowed Winston[2] to meddle in the matter? A piece of interference we look on as an insult? Here is old man Bethell's[3] letter: you can tear it up. I see that two officers, and some men from *Nestor* have been picked up – so young Maurice may be all right.

My poor dear, you are going to have a bad doing. Lou, Willie *and* May! It's a bit thick! Hurry up and get to Warblington – you can let the Egertons[4] have the house? And then they will clear out elsewhere having had enough of Southsea? No more news.

Here is rather a nice story to cheer you up. When Alexander-Sinclair[5] in *Galatea* and Cameron in *Phaeton* brought down that Zepp some weeks ago – Cameron[6] made to his Commodore 'Many Congratulations. Reference Hymn No 224 last verse'.[7]

You look it up! – Yr: C

1. Lord Balfour was First Lord of the Admiralty.
2. Winston (Churchill) First Lord of the Admiralty 1911–15, was forced to resign over the Dardanelles campaign.
3. The Hon Sir Alexander Bethell was C.E. Le M's commanding officer in HMS *Hindustan* 1906-08 and Vice Admiral at the RN War College.
4. Lou and Willie Egerton were C.E. Le M's sister and brother-in-law. May was another sister.
5. Commodore E.S. Alexander-Sinclair commanded HMS *Galatea* and the First Light Cruiser Squadron.
6. Captain J.E. Cameron commanded HMS *Phaeton* in the First Light Cruiser Squadron.
7. Hymn No 224, last verse: 'O happy band of pilgrims
   Look upward to the skies
   Where such a light affliction
   Shall win so great a prize.'

HMS *Hampshire*. Lost off Orkney June 5, 1916 with Lord Kitchener on board.

19

Here is a copy of the offending First Communiqué issued to the Press from the office of Arthur Balfour, First Lord of the Admiralty, on the evening of June 2, 1916.

'On the afternoon of Wednesday May 31, a naval engagement took place off the coast of Jutland. The British ships on which the brunt of the fighting fell were The Battle Cruiser Fleet, and some cruisers and light cruisers supported by four fast battleships. Among those the losses were heavy. The German battle fleet, aided by low visibility, avoided prolonged action with our main forces, and soon after those appeared on the scene, the enemy returned to port, though not before receiving severe damage from our battleships. The Battle Cruisers *Queen Mary*, *Indefatigable*, *Invincible*, and the Cruisers *Defence* and *Black Prince* were sunk. The *Warrior* was disabled, and after being towed for some time, had to be abandoned by her crew. It is also known that the destroyers *Tipperary*, *Turbulent*, *Fortune*, *Sparrowhawk* and *Ardent* were lost and six others are not yet accounted for. No British battleships or light cruisers were sunk. The enemy's losses were serious. At least one battle cruiser was destroyed, and one severely damaged; one battleship reported sunk by our destroyers during a night attack, two light cruisers were disabled and probably sunk. The exact number of enemy destroyers disposed of during the action cannot be ascertained with any certainty, but it must have been large.'

This bald, factual account, probably composed by J.E. Masterton Smith [a civilian secretary (assistant principal) in Balfour's office, and a man innocent of 'spin'] did not emphasise the enemy's hasty flight after Jellicoe arrived. It was so defeatist and resulted in such negative articles that British sailors were hissed by the public on their return. Six hours later the Admiralty corrected the list of destroyer casualties and claimed that a third capital German ship (*Seydlitz*) had sunk in shallow waters (in fact she was only grounded). The Germans, as noted by Le Mesurier, 'kept quiet over their losses that Wednesday night'. The more responsible papers and periodicals, such as 'Land and Water' (June 7, 1916) soon pointed to the enemy's retreat, and asked pertinent questions about safety precautions in British ships' magazines and the thickness of their protective armour. As the British ships had longer range guns than the Germans, thick armour was not deemed necessary, but visibility was poor on May 31 and close-range fighting the order of the day. The Germans fired before the British did at Jutland and their range-finders were more accurate. Above all they stored their cordite more safely.

7. *Saturday 10 June 1916*

Sweetheart – We got in this morning from a trip to a southern base to change our damaged gun. Not bad work, left at 2 p.m. – went down at 20 knots – berthed the little ship alongside a big floating crane – out old and in new, gun. Had a couple of hours sleep, left at 4 o/c and were back here, in our old berth, by 9 a.m. Well under the 24 hours. War has taught our dockyards to work! I found your letter of 6th waiting for me – and rejoiced to think your suspense was over: next time I will send a harmless wire. I thought a p.c. better but it takes too long on the road.

The C-in-C came on board yesterday morning to look at our various scratches and to see the officers and men: he was really most complimentary and kind. I must start whacking out 10A [fatigues] – or they will develop swelled head: the officers have already been put into Harbour Watch! I am getting in the answers from the various relatives I wrote to early in the week. Very plucky, all of them – does one good to read 'em – I *think* – when J.R.J. gets *his* version before the public you will realise that the Germans have no cause to pat themselves on the back – unless that the thick weather and failing light saved them.

Here is another story to cheer you up – On our way South and East that eventful Wednesday, a general signal was made that a certain trawler unit had engaged and sunk a s/m – on the Friday. When we were all busy filling up with coal, oil and ammunition, the S.O of the cruiser squadron sweeping up the North Sea for cripples W/T'd me that he had sunk a s/m by gunfire. Two days later, one of our E. class returned to his base and reported in his account of the cruise that on Wednesday, early, he had fallen in with some armed trawlers who had 'caused him some annoyance' while on Friday night he had 'been seriously discommoded by one of our four-funnel 'cruisers'[1] – Rather nice?

Here is Willie's letter.[2] Probably a good deal in what he says about the non-declaration of war between Italy and Germany & Money does 'talk', as the sailor puts it? 'Tino[3] is in hot water again – and a commercial blockade. A very old remedy for 'hot Greece' is the King.

Heart up. all goes well

Yr.C

---

1. Light cruisers had four funnels, except for the newest models, which had two.
2. W.H. Kirby, Mrs Le M's brother, was a banker in Genoa.
3. King Constantine of Greece.

8. *Sunday 11 June 1916*

A linelet, my Heart, to tell you all goes well, and that I have your letter of 8th, written after my letter of Sunday 4th had reached you – Here is Willie's back. I will see if Martin can take up a lump of stuff for the small son:[1] the said Martin told me last night as he was putting down the dead lights at 9.30 for 'Darken Ship', in answer to my query whether the gig could be mended up 'I counted 150 holes in her!' – I was very cheered to gather yesterday, after we got back here, that the surgeon had been down to the '*China*', hospital ship, during the few hours we were shifting our gun, and that our bad cases were going on very well: they were so groggy that they hadn't been sent South by train: the young bugler boy is the most critical – Rather blowy, but otherwise all right, and that's about all –

The Russians are doing right well. C-in-C told me K.[2] had said that the Germans would not reach their highest point of man-power until *October* of this year, which is some months after the generally accepted estimate. Yep: I think you will find The Old Farm House[3] a very welcome harbourage. I look out of my scuttle and see more Dockyard mateys coming on board with their bags and hammocks – So suspect the First Lieutenant of making a bit out of our necessary repairs. Bless you.

Yr: *C*

1. Edward (Ted) Le Mesurier, b.1903.
2. K: Lord Kitchener (1850–1916) Secretary of State for War.
3. The Old Farm House, Warblington, Hants was rented by Mrs Le Mesurier in August and September 1916. Her landlord was John Green, Captain of HMS *New Zealand*.

The damaged *Calliope* back in Scapa Flow. Photograph probably taken by C.E. Le Mesurier on June 2, 1916. '*Calliope* May 31' is written on the back.

9. *Tuesday 13 June 1916*

Sweetheart. I have yrs: of 9th, and both Lady Poore's book and the box of pinks have arrived in excellent condition. Rather a triumph to have one's own flowers on the table? Get a copy of 'Land and Water' for last week – you will find quite a good account of the big action in it. Pollen's brother, Father Pollen, was our R.C. chaplain in the pre-historic channel fleet Bethell days, and was included in the 'severely wounded'.

We have shifted over to the North Shore to get the men out of the ship: and, incidentally, do some drills. So I am away from the Fleet Flagship and my own callers. The husband of that old camel[1] Armstrong woman was the best man I have ever seen at that game: At Portland, if he couldn't button-hole the Chief of Staff a.m. he would return p.m. – and all for nothing! – A real terror – Martin secured me some fresh souvenirs, so Teddy and Thurston James[2] will be all serene -young monkeys – Yes, they are difficult letters to write. I have had answers now from nearly all of them – very brave – you are such a sympathetic person, my child, that my relations cling to you instinctively! A shocking nuisance, I agree, but look on it as a tribute to your personal charm! At the same time accepting my fullest sympathy. My hat, they *will* quarrel! A combination of Lou, May and Agnes would wreck the Convocation of Canterbury, or whatever the annual meeting of our bishops is called –

No news: I spotted J.R.J. the chief of staff and Halsey[3] all walking up and down on the quarter-deck, and all in the highest spirits, so conclude the dispatches are off their chests! Night-night. Weather simply arctic. Cold N.E.Wind

Yr: *C*

1. Camel night on a warship: women were invited, so this was presumably the night on which you did not get the 'hump', i.e. depressed.
2. Thurston James was a friend of Ted Le M's at the Wells House School, Malvern Wells.
3. Admiral Sir Lionel Halsey was Captain of the Fleet to Admiral Sir John Jellicoe, 1915–16.

'My hat, they *will* quarrel!' Sketch by Hetty *c*.1896.

10. *Wednesday 14 June 1916*

Sweetheart: Just got yrs: of 10th – a letter from the small son, very full of beans, and, to my great content, a long letter from Hal[1], from Cuttack – That blessed godson of mine had cost him some journeying, from Mandalay to Maymo [sic] – Burmah hill station – then on to Simla. The G.O.C. Burmah has been more than good – jumped on the boy with both feet first, and then gave him lots of good advice (Better treatment than Master Arthur would have got out the Royal Navy!). He is to be transferred to a British regiment, where, it is hoped, the senior subaltern will take him in hand. Poor old Hal. He is indeed handicapped?

We are rather disgruntled, having had our holiday on the North Shore cut short by a peremptory order to return to the Fleet anchorage early p.m., so I suppose there is something in the wind. I got a short walk yesterday evening, but will have to put off my promised long tramp.

Hal says he saw Agnes[2] and Jack, and that Agnes ought to come home. Fort Sandeman has tried both of 'em rather high. 'Tis good news from Russia? Crack Austria, and the whole show will come down with a run – The Admiralty have stopped worrying me pro tem: over that Norwegian ship,[3] and I now hope to see her go sailing thro' the Prize court without further delay – There's a lot of trade coming out of, and into, the Baltic now that the ice has melted: the Swedes and Norwegians seem to be running the show well, taking care to escort all ships while in territorial waters.

I saw Admiral Heath yesterday going over to him for tea. He tells me that Lou and Willy were at the wedding of General Heath's daughter t'other day. Otherwise no news and all seems very peaceful. Regular murrain setting into the ship. Officers getting too senior and leaving to better themselves. The new (N) has had bad luck: got pneumonia and so has to drop out. Can't afford to go sick in war time – However he has had a run for his money! Keep you safe and well.   Yr: C

1. Hal (Havilland) Le Mesurier was C.E. Le M's eldest brother, later Sir Havilland, Acting Governor of Bengal.
2. Agnes Gretton (née Le Mesurier). C.E. Le M's youngest sister married an officer in the Indian Army.
3. The *Lökken* was an iron ore ship trading with Germany and captured by C.E. Le M and claimed as a prize.

II. *Thursday 15 June 1916*

Sweetheart I send you my 'dinner-bill' to show you I have been keeping good company of late! H.M. came on board the little ship this morning and walked round – very kind indeed – otherwise not much news, save that mercifully the weather has eased up and 'tisn't so cold. I have had a letter from Tate, but can't give him any details until the despatches come out, probably Saturday or Monday.

There's a regular murrain among Admirals and Captains – and I am simply romping up – believe I am 85 now! To my great joy I saw Ayling this evening. D'you know the man I mean? My chief bosun's mate in *Hindustan* who got disrated over Ross' accident? He told me he had been five years in the same ship and all that time in the same 12in turret! What you might term long service with a vengeance!

The young (N) has had to go and I think I have the pick of the Navigators of our little push coming here. I was very much struck by him when I was in Townsend's[1] ship and rather regretted not having asked for him when Master Colquhoun got the boot, but all is peace now – great comfort having a Navigator you can trust.

And what of the situation? Looks as if the Germans WILL get through to Verdun? At a price? While old man Brussiloff? has undoubtedly eased off the strain on the Italians? I hear K. of K. tell J.R.J. he had two anxieties – the Russians 'who are just like children: give 'em a hundred rounds of ammunition and they will blaze it away' and the Italian front. Here's another war story I heard this afternoon from a brigadier general living on board one of our flagships: His brigade were up in the front trenches. And the usual exchange of messages went on, on boards. 'DON'T SHOOT WE ARE SAXONS' produced a sharp burst of rifle fire from our men. Down went the Germans' board to reappear with 'THANK YOU – YOU HAVE KILLED OUR PRUSSIAN MAJOR'!

And now I must walk. We kept Summer Time while H.M. was with us. And the clocks have gone back, so I am left with time on my hands. Keep you safe and well.

Yr: C

1. Captain C.S. Townsend commanded HMS *Constance*, 4th Light Cruiser Squadron.

12. *Friday 16 June 1916*

Sweetheart I have yrs: of 12th – and send you back Mrs Giffard and the one from Boy Walker's mother. He is rather a bad case, I'm afraid: shell splinter in chest and lung affected, but may pull thro'. All the others are doing very well, we hear, and the Able Seaman who was so badly broken up, will get all right. Mrs Walker will receive allotment and separation allowance for six months – and I should say, some extra help from Prince of Wales' Fund.[1] 'twill take time to settle all these things up. Teddy and Thurston will have had their lumps of stuff by now – Despatches ought to be out early next week – tho' I don't suppose we shall ever hear the true tale of the German losses –

Weather is still arctic, and my fire is going strong, tho' we are in mid-June. I hear the promotions include Barge Goodenough.[2] I've got a lovely story to tell you about him! If so, Frank Ryan is included. Wonder if he will get the bow-string?[3] There will certainly be at least two in the next half dozen who will be told to go – so my prospects of reaching 80 are quite rosy – Not much news, is there? The Russians are helping themselves to more Austrians every day – all to the good, and the Germans still shove on, quite regardless of cost. À Court Repington is about right in the *Times*. 'Tis the next three months to look out for – Our new (N) has joined. I hope very much to get the First Lieutenant promoted – and a D.S.O. for the Staff Surgeon. By the way, if I have any War College stationery, particularly foolscap paper in my den, will you send it along? I get thro' a terrible lot, one way and another and have run out to a clinch. We certainly used to waste an awful lot of paper at that Hot Air depôt! Wonder if I shall ever get back there? They will certainly want a trained staff to write the naval side of the war – at present we are only getting letters in the papers? And damn silly ones at that. Shall never be sufficiently thankful that we got back here – safe from prying Press men and other distracting influences?

Night-night

Yr: C

1. Pensions, sick pay and death benefit needed attention; the Great War gave impetus to social policy.
2. Commodore William Goodenough RN, Captain of HMS *Southampton* and the Second Light Cruiser Squadron.
3. To get the bow-string: be fired!

13. *Sunday 18 June 1916*

Sweetheart – What shall I tell you about? Nothing doing up here – and I am suffering from a heavy lunch and, being emergency ship, can't go ashore to walk it off. Thanks be the wind is falling off and we no longer shake and shiver. I have yr: letter of 14th and await, with some anxiety? your impressions of Lou! Sooner you can get to Warblington the better – The Flag List changes are most interesting – and exciting. No list of Captains promoted has yet appeared, probably 'cos the victims 'desired' to retire are still wriggling. Ryan, I am told, is one – Rumour has it that Masterton Smith, one of the two civilian secretaries to the First Sea Lord – was answerable for that Admiralty communiqué that Friday night. Boiling oil plus the boot – clearly indicated – Now remains to look out for the C-in-Chief's yarn.

    I read out the King's Message after church today: rather discomposed, as the last hymn, a very ordinary shanty shanty one, was unbeknownst apparently to the sailors, as well as the organist, and so found myself performing a solo, only supported by the raucous treble of the young Assistant Clerk! Rather interested in my Admiralty correspondence now as I am fighting them over several points. Both Engineer[1] officers got scrubbed over the fire below last March: they have deprived one of our men of his long service medal most unjustly and have appointed a Lieutenant (G)[2] here without saying a word. Conspiracy! Old Dexter writes that he is still short of pay – probably hospital stoppages – and wants to come back but he wouldn't last thro' the winter up here – besides the vacancy is filled – otherwise my mail is blank. I am having rows with the Dockyard men on board and shall probably, much against the grain, have to run 'em in – Anyhow shall refuse to sign any overtime sheets. Ain't I becoming a perfect model of integrity? Night-night – all goes well.

Yr: C

1. An example of Engineer officers being blamed by superiors who lacked specialised knowledge of engineering.
2. G: Gunnery. These officers enjoyed high status; even the commander of the 4th L.C.S. was not consulted about this appointment.

14. *Monday 19 June 1916*

Sweetheart: No news, and there's nothing whatever doing – winds very strong yesterday and today, now, evening-time, backing off -and that's about all I have to tell you. A big batch of promotions, I make myself 84 – and both Da Costa and Grafton are bound to be retired on promotion so I shan't be long! Goodenough is an Admiral – 11½ years seniority and just 49 – I wonder very much what they will do with him: he has been three years in *Southampton*. Russians are doing wonders: Wilhelm and his advisers must be thinking hard.

Isn't it curious to read of food riots in Holland? The Dutch, Danes, Swedes and Norwegians have all literally battened on the war, coined money and they have the neck on 'em, like the Yanks, to blame our blockade! De Chair[1] has done a lot of good work since he went adviser to the F.O. Haven't heard anything more about our ORE ship, but hope to see ship and cargo safely condemned – We are all tolerably cheerful, tho' for myself, I find this long spell at anchor – 'tis getting on for three weeks now, rather trying: probably due to being too much on board. The weather has been against landing – Never mind we are off to the North Shore on Thursday, and this time I hope no BIG BUGS will come up to try *Calliope* back to the Fleet anchorage! tho' 'tis very ungrateful to talk like that seeing how gracious H.M. was – The sailor son[2] in *Collingwood* looks twice the man his elder brother of Wales[3] is – Not unlike George and *his* elder brother, the Duke of Clarence.

We are very busy working out schemes to give us additional protection from the stray shell splinter on it's way below: all I hope is that My Lords will remember that the speed of these little ships is their principal safe-guard, and won't overload 'em – you can't have everything in this world and you certainly cannot make a four thousand ton fast light cruiser into a vessel capable of standing up to armoured ships! Now I must go and harry the Dockyard workmen! Night-night All goes well

Yr: C

1. Admiral Sir Dudley de Chair was naval adviser at the Ministry of Blockade 1916–17.
2. Prince Albert, later George VI.
3. Prince Edward, later King Edward VIII, who abdicated 10 December, 1936.

Muirhead Bone, R.A. *Cold sailor on ship in Scapa Flow*. Arctic weather conditions, even in mid June, led Le Mesurier to 'walk up and down after dinner with my duffel coat on and tramp to keep myself warm.' *(Imperial War Museum 1357)*

15. *Tuesday 20 June 1916*

Sweetheart I have yr: letter of 16th. What a quite heavenly story! but 'Mum's the word'. You seem to be having a bad time with my side of the family relations! Willy very much, and Lou as well, I'm afraid, have no sense of decency when it comes to getting other people to do their work. 'Tis rather more marked in Anglo-Indians than in people who have not lived out there.

I found myself in a terrible scrape last night – a Service letter asking me when an answer might be expected, and found the screed in question buried a foot deep in my 'AWAIT' basket! Result, a cold towel round my head all day. Otherwise no news, and 'tis dull work swinging round one's anchor. Just as well it's not two anchors! as we used to in the winter – This icy cold can't go on for always, makes one long to be South, reading of the children having tea in the garden. I walk up and down after dinner with my duffel coat on, and tramp to keep myself warm – Mid-June too.

What of the War? I hear leave is stopped, so we may hear of something coming on, over there – Parliament again tomorrow, not that that is much of a catch! The Germs: are sitting very tight over their losses on the 31st. Kiel and Wilhelmshaven wired in and the telephones cut to Denmark and Holland. No doubt about it but that they are very thorough. We have probably allowed dozens of enemy agents to have a good look at our ships under repair. Walter Allen had a near shave, good bit of work to get his ship in at all. My conscience is at ease once more as I have screwed myself up and run the Dockyard mateys in!

Night-night, my Heart. All goes well.

Yr: C

16. *Wednesday 21 June 1916*

Sweetheart. I have yrs: of 18th: Did I never tell you about the cake? How ungrateful of me, for it has nearly disappeared! What shall I recount to you of H.M.'s visit? He paid us one very great compliment, as, after looking at the representative detachments from this ship – and the others of the squadron, all drawn up in a line, he walked round the remainder of our ship's company – He looked at our various holes and so on, and then I took him thro' my cabin to look at our 'souvenirs'. Lasted about half-an-hour – Our W/T tells us that Jellicoe and Beatty are promoted in the Victorian Order, so perhaps the despatches may be out. Promotions at the end of the month ought to be rather interesting?

Woodrow Wilson seems to have struck resolution at last, tho' 'tis only against Mexico – To call out the militia in the United States is very like mobilisation over here: they usually temporise with men of war – so as not to disturb the dollar grinding. Roosevelt's dictum that 'our country is becoming a polyglot boarding-house where dollar hunters of twenty different nationalities scramble for gain' is caustic but not far off the mark? I hope another piece of W/T news is correct – that one result of the conference in Paris has been a determination to screw up the blockade of Germany: use our Naval power properly and much will come.

All this very petty 'rationing' of Denmark, Holland and so on – letting 'em have cotton, oils, and so on – on an average of three years' imports – only means the stuff goes into Germany, and the Dane or Dutchman goes short. Witness the recent food riots in Holland! Hang up the cargoes, and don't release them, and we must break the Germans. 'Tis all very fine for the respective neutral Governments to forbid export. We know very well what can be done by greasing palms and wholesale smuggling – while as to neutral feeling? They have had two years to coin money in – Well, well. No doubt we could run the show very much better up here!

Night-night – Yr: C

17. *Tuesday 24 June 1916*

Sweetheart. Better news this morning: German line pierced in ten places and a great Italian victory reported?[1] Looks as if things were really, really, beginning to move. We had quite a good three or four hours yesterday, running about after a target – and that is really all I have to tell you! See what a dull, if healthy life it is! The tale of the German losses at sea is slowly mounting up: I hope six big ships of theirs have gone. Very hard to get news tho'.

How goes with my relations? And does Warblington seem any closer? Very soon now we will start July? And you move out at the end? I am rather wondering whether John Green will try for any of the shore jobs vacant thro' promotion? Portland, Chatham Dockyard, a Coast-guard Captaincy are three of them – The prospect of a third winter is not over-alluring? I hear C-in-C's despatches have been a whole week at the Admiralty: I hope 'tis not so, as it would mean that My Lords are editing them, and they will certainly make a mess of it!

I am still getting letters from the nearest relatives: very plucky, and all exceedingly grateful to you, so you did well, my chick – The Dockyardmen should clear out in a couple of days: the new gang, for I had the old lot turfed out, have done more work in a week than their predecessors did in twenty days – Lazy devils, and all getting double pay for being up here! No doubt about it, payment by results is the game. All our horny-handed ones, and for the matter of that, our soft-handed ones as well, will have to work a jolly sight harder for some years to come. I am standing by for many defect and alteration lists for my little ships. Now is the time to profit by what we have learnt, once the main repairs have been tackled.

Night-night, all goes well and smoothly

Yr: *C*

1. The German line was pierced at Verdun; the Austrian lines by the Italians in Trentino, Northern Italy.

18. *Saturday 24 June 1916*

Sweetheart. I have yrs: of 20th and here is Atta's card back – Bless her! – And so you have my family descended on you? Hurry up the next five weeks and send you safe harbourage at The Old Farm House! 'Tis easy to walk round and vent one's spleen, but a different pair of shoes when one has to catch a train! So glad the Mouse seems resigned to her new foot-gear: 'twas an experiment how she would take 'em. Here all is peace: I had a topping good walk yesterday, landed at 9 o/c and climbed to the top of a hill: did me a lot of good. In the afternoon we ran torpedoes – to my relief they behaved themselves, and this morning I should have gone on shore again but was swamped out with paper-work. It really is the curse of modern life afloat.

My summer pants, *con rispetto*, resemble my under outfit in 1900![1] More holes than garments, but I can make shift all right.

I am 80 or 81 now, not quite certain which. Power. Captain Superintendant Tyne is the man to go to to push me on to affluence and payment of my debts. What of the news? We had a special Press message, unofficial, t'other day, that Hindenburg had been severely knocked, but I fear me 'twas a case of the Will, and not the deed – on the whole though, things are going on well. We must be getting ready, for I hear all leave from France is stopped – Rather amusing Shackles Corbett getting a D.S.O. What with that, and Tubby Lockyer's C.B. all tho, what shall I say? – less blameless members of the post-captains' list have been decorated. I heard a most delightful phrase about a certain rather talkative brother senior officer of one of our light cruiser squadrons – 'He talked very loud at first but he is better now!' Made me chuckle – even at 6.30 a.m.

Night-night, my Heart

Yr: *C*

---

1. Possibly a reference to the state of his underwear in March 1900, when he married!

19. *Sunday 25 June 1916*

Sweetheart: I have yrs: of 22nd and here is the small son's back – I also am the richer for a great fat cake, one of *Caroline*'s masterpieces, as well as quite a lot of scribbling paper so I am well off. I should be able to see the war through on my loot from the War College! Curiously enough it is one of the bones of contention between C.O. and Accountant officer, who is to supply service writing paper. The Paymaster, and the Secretary, get a quarterly allowance for stationery – and don't forget to keep the Captain (or distinguished Flag officer) on an allowance! Of course one really has the bulge on 'em,[1] 'cos they can't get their allowance until the Captain signs, but there it is – Curiously enough, Smyth, when senior of the office in the old Cotton Wool[2] days, much resented my sending in to him for scribbling paper!

Smyth, by the way, is very cock-a-whoop as he has been made Acting Paymaster on the strength of a letter containing a larger modicum of truth than my Service letters are usually flavoured with, re his prospects. The Admiralty are rather tame just now: I have got three or four things I have asked for. Eh, my dear, we've got to take our relations as we find 'em! My only hope is that I shall age with decency – Willie is a 'miss-fire' as the sailors say.

Not so cold, but very foggy. I suppose we shall get summer some time? Told you about my under clo' – didn't I? And am sending you a parcel of socks, as I have plenty of good new ones. News continues on the good side: Wilhelm has apparently gone East, and they seem to be taking men away from their western front. Now is our time to push them – I much hope we shall get some activity at sea: this month has seemed terribly long, doing nothing. Regular got up washed and went to bed business. However, the sailors have now had an outing and are fairly cheery, so that's all right.

Night-night, my Heart, all goes well and smoothly

Yr: *C*

1. Has the bulge on 'em: has an advantage over them.
2. Old Cotton Wool: possibly Sir Michael Culme-Seymour (retired March 1901) in the Channel Fleet.

Enclosures:

(1) WHEN TORPEDO MEETS TORPEDO

A Guildford telegraphist, who was aboard a light cruiser during the naval battle, relates the following remarkable incident: – His ship was considerably damaged and was dropping out of action when the Germans fired a torpedo.

'It would probably have caught the cruiser amidships,' says the telegraphist, 'but another British vessel fired at, hit and exploded the torpedo before it reached the cruiser. It was a wonderfully lucky shot for us.'

(2) *WARSPITE*'S 'SALMON'

The Rev. Forbes Phillips, of Gorleston, speaking at the meeting of the St. Andrew's Waterside Mission, held at Church House yesterday, related an experience of a sailor who was present at the Jutland battle.

'We saw some funny things,' said the sailor. 'The guns were ear-splitting, but I was sure I could hear a lot of men laughing. When I asked what they were laughing at, one replied, "Look at the old *Warspite*!" She was careering through the water with a German submarine hooked right up to her ram. It was like a big dog with a salmon in its mouth.'

20. *Wednesday 28 June 1916*

Sweetheart. I have yrs: of 24th with the enclosure from the 'Financier on the Hard'. Don't 'ee worry, my dear, you have quite enough hay on your fork as it is – and I always proposed to devote my extra five bob per diem (I haven't got it yet!) to liquidating over-draft Army & Navy Stores and Outfitter.

Am so cheered they have made Arthur Ross an acting Commander at last. The Italians seem really, all right, and have made a very good recovery. I wonder much whether this is the real 'Push'! Up here no news – we are bombarded every day with new returns to fill up and new reports to tender. Gad, my dear, did you but see my basket a.m. and p.m. with it's papers and buggins, you wouldn't wonder at my longing to get out of touch with the Admiralty and C-in-C. Just now we are all trying to benefit by our experiences that Wednesday evening – and the many committees sitting, refer questions relating to light cruisers to me, so 'tis more than usual, just now – but, but. We are really developing into BABU'S – 'Behests of honour and chivalry alike'.

Cheer up, my chick, a short month and you will be shut, pro tem of my relatives! 'Tis much lucky we have always had several thousand miles of salt sea between us!

With such a cold and cheerless June, July and August must surely compensate? My fire is still kept going – There's a big local[1] outbreak of measles reported in the town where our stewards go marketing – so we shall probably be cut off from what flesh pots are handy. Some men brought a haul of cod alongside this evening – and disposed of 'em in a very few minutes.

Night-night
Yr: C

1. Kirkwall, Orkney.

Muirhead Bone, R.A. *HMS Queen Elizabeth's guns in fog.* Although *Queen Elizabeth* (5th Battle Squadron) missed Jutland as she was having a refit at the time, this picture shows how long range guns lost their advantage in poor visibility. *(Imperial War Museum 1345)*

21. *Thursday 29 June 1916*

Sweetheart: I have yrs. here is Willie's back and a couple of tall stories sent by Nellie-Nell to cheer you and the Mouse – It's rather nice to think of the authority of the Church being given to what is perhaps the biggest 'banker' of the War! A dreary day, raining hard, may bring us a much needed change. Except that the Admiralty telegraph that the announcement of the promotions will be delayed, there is no news. There was a very serious letter from Professor Mahaffy in yesterday's *Times* about giving Ireland even modified Home Rule just now, so Lord Selborne may be right in leaving the Government, only he should have done so before? Wonder if it <u>is</u> true that the R.C.'s are against Home Rule as they think they will lose their hold on the Irish? They are certainly doing their best to keep the pot boiling by masses for the dead and so on.

I have been again spoiling a lot of good paper this afternoon, and that's about all – we are getting quite veterans in *Calliope* now: this time last year we had waddled as far as Devonport – our third breakdown. I lunched there with the Munby's, Dockyard Admiral and well remember Mrs Admiral Superintendant's pessimism 'Think of their asphyxiating gases' was one of her contributions to the gaiety of the meal! That reminds me that the Admiralty have served out some very practical goggles. Somebody sent me up a letter and typed 'experiences' from Percy Royds, you know, big house on hill? I had to read 'em over two or three times before I could take his yarn in – and can only charitably suppose he wrote the screed for consumption in the nursery. Nellie-Nell says they have come across a midshipman who was in control top of *Barham*.[1] My word that boy must be spreading himself at Pinner! Makes an old bird like myself long to be in his place! What shall we say '*Si la vieillesse pouvait!*'[2] but I am getting ribald.

Night-night. All is peaceful –
Yr: C

---

1. HMS *Barham*, flagship of Rear-Admiral Hugh Evan-Thomas, led the 5th Battle Squadron in the Battle Cruiser Fleet of four fast battleships (24 knots). She had eight 15-inch guns, a 13-inch armour belt and displaced 27,000 tons.
2. '*Si la jeunesse savait, si la vieillesse pouvait.*' 'If youth only knew; if age only could!'

A foretop officer wearing gas mask and fighting equipment. 'The Admiralty have served out some very practical goggles' *(Imperial War Museum Q17937)* Le Mesurier reassured his wife in this letter.

22. *Friday 30 June 1916*

Sweetheart: A Happy Month to you and speedy deliverance from my side of the family! Warblington will do you good – and surely, surely we shall see Summer soon? I send you back young Hopeful's screed: his place in class is all right if his cricket is a bit racky? No news here, damp wet fog and what wind there is from the North. I am very cheered to read what you say about the Mouse's *pluck*, for to have a child of her own age, a stranger, to watch and not to grow jealous of, is a very great test. Eh, my dear, we must be patient, brave and not lose hope. Remember this, that had it not been for you, our child would not be where she is now. No hireling, not even our priceless Nannie, would have got her on so far – There is good vitality – she is growing, is healthy, thanks be, and it may come about yet, tho' we must face a difference in length. At Devonport, R. B. Farquhar told me one of his daughters, a fine strapping young woman, was at one time laid out for six long years – Let us have courage then, and not grow faint-hearted, even tho' the top of the hill be not yet in sight. Bless you.

News continues on the good side. The Italians make progress – the Russians add to their bag – and we are hammering the German trenches flat – while those marvellous Frenchmen rise superior to every attack. Much is to be looked for from the abandonment of the Declaration of London – or rather what is left of it. I'm bound to own up that what I looked on as a good working compromise has failed miserably: we live and learn, tho' no one contemplated sinking merchant vessels with submarines. I hope to see a real blockade declared, which will give us a real grip on neutral trade, and so materially reduce Germany's resources. 'Tis the time now, before she can gather in the crops.

Be of good cheer

Yr: *C*

23. *Sunday 2 July 1916*

Sweetheart: No news save that [of] the great and glowing announcements from our front in Flanders: it really does look more like the real thing, at last? Must be authentic as we had two or three extra Press W/T from Admiralty. To hammer in the German front for a width of 70 [sic] miles is good work.[1] I had a much needed tramp yesterday: came across Master Lane who is Flag Captain, very busy gardening in front of a cottage helping a youngish female person. Off went my cap 'How d'you do, Mrs Lane, and how d'you like this after Rowlands Castle'? Turned out to be a Mrs Somebody Quite Different! Still raw and uncomfy: my fire looks like to burn all round the clock of 1916. A long letter from old Tyrwhitt[3]: I have spent this afternoon sending him a screed. He tells me he pushed out on getting the wireless, that Wednesday evening, on his own! And got properly scrubbed by the Admiralty! I wish, I wish My Lords would hurry up with *their* version of the fight and announce the promotions. What on earth are they waiting for? Old man Tirpitz isn't likely to send over a full and detailed account yet awhile? Neither are we to be gratified with a proof copy of the Naval General Staff version! That reminds me that I bumped into Eustace Long[2] yesterday and sends you salutes. And so Lloyd George is Minister for War: there is the future Prime Minister. Winston is out of court. There's a cold breeze of doubt playing over the Irish business now: 'pon my word, one doesn't know what to think? Let'em stew in their own juice for a bit, and chance having to put down another big rising? Or keep 'em under with martial law? Both methods expensive – Let's get on with downing the Hun, anyway – We have rather a busy week coming, quite a good thing, as we have all sorts of trials to carry out, and a light cruiser is just the sort of fancy toy ship they like to play with. Keeps one going, anyhow. All goes well
Night-night
Yr: *C*

1. It is sad to see this misreport of the first day of the Battle of the Somme.
2. Eustace Long was a relation by marriage to Mrs Le M.
3. Commodore Reginald Tyrwhitt commanded The Harwich Force, and was ordered back to base by Vice-Admiral Oliver. 'It would have been of enormous help . . . if Tyrwhitt had been available to watch the Horn's Reef route, but thanks to the malign influence of Oliver, the Harwich force was in its base.' Julian Thompson p. 314 *The Imperial War Museum Book of the War at Sea 1914–1918*. The High Seas Fleet limped back to port via the Horn's Reef, the only route not covered by the Grand Fleet.

24. *Monday 3 July 1916*

Sweetheart – yrs: of 30th with Arthurs's – I have just written him. My dear, had you seen that last letter he sent me, soon after he got the push from his Gurkha battalion you would realise what a difference! Low diet and a few salutary twinges of conscience have worked wonders – let us hope this chastened frame of mind will continue?

I am afraid that young bugler boy Walker is very groggy. Our men have fetched up at Chatham Hospital, and we have good accounts of all, save of him. I wrote Lady Callaghan about them on Saturday, also to Bowden Smith who is now Flag Captain there. You might write to the Chaplain, R.N.H. Chatham? Or Head Sister, a Miss Margaret Keenan R.R.C. The Admiralty have again gone off their rocker and have given me a young Signal Officer, a certain Lieutenant Bottomley. I hope no relation to 'John Bull'? Do they imagine *Calliope* is elastic? I have five officers as it is, slinging a hammock, and don't want to give up Lieutenant (T). When I move, when *Calliope* has to dock, I shall have to travel with Secretary, Lt:(T) Lt:(S) clerk, Bos (S), Warrant Telegraphist, plus writer, Coxswain, four stewards and a cook. How's that for a modest man? I had forgotten two signal ratings. 15 all told?

Had a great skylark this morning: made a signal to land every available man an average of 200 per ship, doubled two miles and off again. We have had some running about and are now on our beloved North Shore, so I look forward to climbing a hill tomorrow – Yes, get little Marge to look up Mrs Walker and report on her circumstances. If the boy does go out I might be able to work a grant from our Grand Fleet Fund – now well on it's legs, or the Admiralty –

Night-night, all goes well, very well

Yr: C

T = Torpedo
S = Signals

25. *Thursday 6 July 1916*

Sweetheart. How goes? I do believe we are really going to have some fine weather at last! As cold and dismal a June and first week July as ever I have seen. I have yrs: of lst. Yep: 1 June was a day of many emotions. I fully thought and hoped to have another smack at 'em, early daylight, for to be quite frank, the opportunities missed on that Wednesday evening were a-many: Here had come <u>the</u> opportunity of all; what one had seen, once the main fleets got into touch, gave no cause for anything but absolute confidence: their great asset destroyer attacks in large numbers had not been developed to anything like the extent we had anticipated – and, once hit, their gunnery went to pieces. All the omens were good – and yet – as the day wore on, and we swept backwards and forwards on our track of the day before, one realised, bitterly, that they had given us the slip.

My little push passed thro' a whole heap of debris about 8 a.m. Oil – life buoys, dead bodies, relics of one of our many destroyer attacks – you will get the Naval despatches tomorrow and probably the promotions: we hope to have 'em tonight by W/T – The Honours come out later. I had a wire telling me to forward a revised list increasing my number of recommends.

The news from France is quite good, and we are holding our own. The Russians are smacking at Hindenburg too, so Wilhelm is fully occupied just now – May he continue to be so! I say, what must Birrell[1] feel like? Pretty stinking report, but these politicians have thick hides. If a fellow in the Government Service makes a mistake, down he goes, but a Cabinet Minister can be as incompetent or as lazy as he pleases, and nothing happens; indeed he is cheered sympathetically by his fellow toadies in Parliament because he owns up he has made an ass of himself! I will let you know if Lady Callaghan writes, how that boy Walker is getting on. Have heard no gossip for quite a long time: comes of being over on the North Shore, tho' 'twas not time wasted, as I got two good walks in.

Night-night. Keep a stout heart. All goes well
yr: C

---

1. Augustine Birrell (1850–1933) Chief Secretary for Ireland 1907–16, resigned after the Easter Rising, May 11, 1916.

26. *Saturday 8 July 1916*

Sweetheart: I have yrs: of 5th and here is the young monkey's back: What is his phrase 'Rocks and giblets'? However, my dear, if his writing, like mine, requires 'careful consideration', what d'you think of Thurston's, as per enclosed? It arrived with a Malvern postmark and a legible address so I surmise Mrs James has been paying the Wells House a visit and gone to General Quarters with her young hopeful? I have had a letter from Lou, and pulled her leg in reply. Only hope she won't treat you to a *sfagata* in consequence! We are getting on thro' July and Warblington is coming nearer? Jellicoe's despatches bear signs of careful editing for public consumption: made me rather sick! The situation certainly called for very careful description. Very cheered to hear from Lou that she will probably use the house. By the way, our young Lieutenant (T) left yesterday to go thro' a course at Portsmouth, starting Monday – only four days. He will probably get hold of his wife – Phillips is the name. I have asked him to give you our news. If they come, give 'em hospitality – Army and Navy will send in drinks – I told him we had a spare room for Mrs Phillips, but think he murmured Queen's Hotel.

Had quite a good afternoon's play round yesterday: torpedoes all behaved themselves and we then took each other in tow, for practice. By the way, that towing of one destroyer by another, mentioned in the despatch, was a very fine piece of work. The sun is out and yet Martin has insisted on lighting my fire. However, he is not VERY reliable as a weather expert. The Germans seem to be regaining some of the ground our fellows carried, but at the expense of rushing up reserves, and the news of riots in Berlin is most encouraging. We must set our teeth and keep at 'em.

Night-night. All goes well
Yr: C

Robert H Smith RNVR: *The Battle of Jutland. Admiral Jellicoe arrives with the battleships and meets the cruisers. (Imperial War Museum 1225)*

27. *Sunday 9 July 1916*

Sweetheart: How goes? Summer told a flattering tale this a.m. wind light southerly breezes and a glorious sun, but not for long, as our noses are pointing North again and the thermometer on it's way to zero. I got the full tale of C-in-C's despatches from the *Times* – and am sending you, for the archives, the official edition sent me from Admiralty, a replica. What I *should* like to see would be the real, Service, account, only that is not made public. I am very comforted, as I get quite unbiassed confirmation from David Beatty's report that an explosion *did* occur in the enemy's line at the time our torpedo was due to cross their track, and as no-one happened to be firing at 'em just then, it is quite possible those ten men of my little *Calliope* were not thrown away? I told C-in-C when I saw him on the day we got back – that Friday 2nd – that it was a 'possible', only that I was very modest about it – But oh dear me! The opportunities lost! Well, well, let us wait for next time – otherwise no news. The new Navy list puts me 81, so the next promotion admits me to the inner circle. Hasn't taken long to romp thro' the second 80? tho' it seems years since I came home from *Highflyer*!

My Service family is to be added to quite soon,[1] probably by the end of the month. We shall be quite saucy then! The 'War on Land' seems to go well for us? My word, what fine fellows they are! That Ulster Division! And the Lancashire men! Let us take our hats off to the British infantry. We should get the promotions soon, this week as ever is, I hope, and then a Gazette. After that I hope we shall resume business, 'tis high time we showed a leg.

Night-night, my Heart Yr: *C*

1. By HMS *Cambrian*.

28. *Friday 14 July 1916*

Sweetheart: We have been Hun-hunting since Monday – only getting back last night, so I am a bit adrift with my mails – and hasten to make your letter the 'early bird and worm' for the day, as once four days Service mail, plus diary of events, is let loose on me, there is no leisure knocking about. My dear, you have my 'symperfy'. I never had much use for my talkative brother in law – tho' he never got on my nerves. True, I haven't seen much of him: probably he would? I remember Hal and he nearly coming to blows at Cuttack, that Xmas. He is intolerably selfish, and, in his own line, a failure. Also, in Anglo-Indian life, it is nothing out of the way to lend, or occupy, other people's houses: let that go in his favour. Comes of having large troops of servants.

Cheer up, Warblington in a fortnight! Yep, my chick, I should much like the four walls of the den and yourself as the only 'assistance' while I let rip about that Wednesday evening and night! but it can't be done on paper in these hard times. Not much – Let us look on it as a good (and satisfactory) Dress Rehearsal! So cheered to hear from the Mouse: thank her and the Babies very warmly. Martin continues to flourish!

The Huns seem to have done rather well to get that craft over to Baltimore? It is significant, my dear, that Wilhelm is reduced to writing surreptitiously to the only two important neutrals left – and we shall get a tighter grip on him now that the blockade has been screwed up. Still – we have another winter to get thro' – And you were pleased, my Heart, with what J.R.J. said? I am very glad he put that little sentence in about my Captains, for they were superlative in their handling of their ships. The lesson of all this long and weary wait has been that you MUST leave things to individual initiative in these very high-speed little ships – there is no time to make signals – and I am very pleased with the way my few 'Action' signals were taken in, and acted on.

Bless you. I put my nose to the grindstone!

Hug 'em all

Yr: *C*

Muirhead Bone, R.A. *The Fleet Post Office.* The official war artist appointed in 1916 to the Grand Fleet in Scapa Flow saw the P.O.'s significance in Orkney. Postage cost a penny, and hundreds of thousands of letters passed through this ramshackle hut on stilts to loved ones at home. *(Imperial War Museum 1782)*

29. *Saturday 15 July 1916*

Sweetheart. Cheer up, and look at the date. Warblington in a fortnight! I have been polishing off back mails. Wish you would ask May how I am to address Lem:?[1] He wrote me on 8th from a training school for officers. Otherwise no news: still cold and misty. For the first time since we have been up here I had occasion to ask for the weather conditions off the entrance. We were romping home at 22 knots and ran into a thick fog bank about 50 miles out – Got the answer when we were well inside! but Hush! News continues good – we are pushing on methodically which is everything – and, wonders will never cease! They have given up the August holidays. We are really waking up. I hear the promotions are delayed until 1st August. They had better make a job of it and put 'em off until 1/April/1917? 'Tis very hard on those who have acute promotion fever. Good news from Chatham. All our cases are doing well, and that boy Walker is up and in the verandah – They took a piece of shrapnel $2\frac{1}{2}$ ozs: out of that leading signalman's shoulder – No chance of any retirements apparently. Sydney Fre(mantle): goes afloat on his own – and that's about all the gossip I have picked up – That German submarine trader[2] isn't as big as was first made out. A tidy good effort all the same. He will have an anxious time on his way home. If I belonged to his ship's company I should bank the bounty money received over there!

Heart up. All goes well

Yr: *C*

1. Lem: Charles Le Mesurier's nephew, son of his eldest brother Havilland (Hal).
2. *Deutschland.*

30. *Thursday 20 July 1916*

Sweetheart. We are becoming regular Ulysses. What is that delightful line in Phillips' *Ulysses*? 'Storm-tossed toilers of the weary main' No: but something like it – J.R.J. has had us out for some most interesting P.Z.'s[1] – well worth watching, and bar fog, F.O.G. with a vengeance: couldn't see 200 yards as we came in at 18 knots (Nothing like having the C-in-C just behind one, to harden one's heart!) – this morning – toppin' fine weather. *Calliope* has arrived, ever so merry. She will look real well on my white spaces, tho' one side, since you were on board is taken up with a very business like chart of the North Sea.[2]

About my intimate garments, my child. I *should* like some thin pants – long leggers – and some more cholera belts – say three of each. Am really very well off for thick things, and I will get myself another woolly waistcoat up here. Yrs: of 17th to greet me. I send you back some of the letters. Yes: I admired the small son's business-like admission! We must keep the stiff upper lip, my Heart and wait until we have downed the Hun, and then my cached hit will 'make a hive for bees' – good lines those, see your '*Newcomes*'[3] for them – and such good news about Atta – Also so cheered you have had a quack with someone decent! No promotions yet: 'tis rather hard on those concerned. As for yourselves, Warblington is almost 'next week' – and nothing else matters, does it?

I have had two letters from Chatham. Bowden Smith wrote all our people are getting on well, and are being well looked after. Bowden Smith doesn't seem to fancy Flag Captain, and leaves soon. He says he got ten days 'blowing-up leave' out of the Admiralty. There should be a good many changes round before long if only to find employment for the young Captains at the Admiralty, who have had an eye on the new ships coming along, and who will get relieved by the men stepped up from Commander. We seem to be pushing along slowly but surely on the Somme – and have attracted a whole heap of Germans, which is all to the good of the cause.

Night-night. I go to my paper-work

Yr: *C*

1. P.Z.'s: tactical exercises.
2. This must be a reference to a picture or photograph of the ship given by Foffs to go on the white spaces of Le Mesurier's cabin bulkhead. Since Foffs visited him on board ship the North Sea chart has been put up on the opposite bulkhead.
3. *The Newcomes* by William Thackeray.

31. *Friday 21 July 1916*

Sweetheart. We are romping thro' the month, thanks to having lots of time at sea: June was drefful slow in going, and 'tis but a little more than a week now that you will be at blessed Warblington. I prophesy you real good weather – Nothing here: we had a big 'pow-wow' in J.R.J.'s fore cabin this morning: I thought some of the Serene Transparencies present were coming to blows! And old Everett, dear old Ev: has rolled up on a visit. Looks rather white and Admiralty atmosphere-y, but his tongue hasn't lost any bite! Don't think I hanker after polishing an office stool in that building – and yet, we once nearly went there, didn't we? News continues on the good side? I have mislaid my copy of the *Morning Liar* – for we get two Press messages now – but it was quite hopeful. Otherwise all is fairly quiet and peaceful – we hope to bring our regatta off early next month – and the sailors go away fairly often boat-pulling. Great problem that, question of exercise – I had a real brain wave t'other day: instituted a sort of Marathon race – land at one pier and double over a mile to another pier, first ship to get her men back breaking the 'one' pendant, gets over 200 men per ship on shore, great skylark – My old *Highflyer* friend, now chaplain of the Fleet Flagship, came over to see me this morning: it seems our little Squadron padré wants more help (Doesn't sound well for the moral tone of the outfit, does it?) and had been to see him. Hope I have pacified them both, but told them they must get bigger ships – or how can I do it? I must have a look at my new ugly duckling, when she arrives, and go into ways and means. Too many people pulling all ways at Charles E! – Night-night, my Heart – all goes well. Yr: *C*

46

32. *Saturday 22 July 1916*

Sweetheart: Such a heavenly morning! And all's well with the world. We are going outside in an hour for a long-range shoot so I have pulled myself out of bed and devoured my brekker well ahead of routine time. Something to be said for daylight saving? Yrs: of 19th came last night, so this is the last letter to Helena Road for what I hope will be two very happy months for you and the chicks – so be it. Yes. Willie Egerton is a bit of a cough-drop and doesn't mellow with age, more's the pity. Think of that garden and the field, and those nice people all round you: even old Norris with the good heart – they will all welcome you. Yep: Muchly would I like to join you! but what would you? Never mind. When all this bother and worry is happily over we will settle down in the country – WEST side of the Malvern Hills! And I will grow roses and sweet peas – and you shall have a chicken run plus a cow. And we will watch the Mouse and Alice and Anne grow up like the 'polished corners of the temple' (there will be lots of surface about Anne to be 'clean wood and bright work'?) and we will forget 1914/1917 – but we must attend to Wilhelm first – There is a very good article by Cope Cornford in the *National Review* for July. Worth reading, if you get the chance, while the current *Spectator* article on Jellicoe's despatches is also quite sound and soberly worded. Yes – I do trust, next time we meet those gentlemen, that the Admiralty, whether Civil Side or Naval Side, will not make such consummate idiots of themselves – and begin by a public apology! Still no promotions: they must be wrangling a lot among themselves up at head quarters – Nine o/c and 'tis time to think about getting the anchor up: the other ships are on the move.

Bless you,

Yr: *C*

The broadside mess deck of a light cruiser. Sailors ate, lived and slept in this crowded space. The scuttle on the left is open for fresh air; the bars above the tables are for slinging hammocks. H.M.S. *Calliope*'s overall width was only 41.5ft. (*Imperial War Museum* Q18676)

33. *Sunday 23 July 1916*

Sweetheart. 'Moths' not by Ouida make me break thro' my resolve NOT to address you any more, pro: tem – at Soufsea [sic]. Bung 'em all to the Belgians, my dear – Save the uniform – you might send me up one pair of the Buncrana bags [Donegal tweed trousers], and my brown shoes – ? – 'tis a good kit to go walking in and saves on uniform pantaloons and boots. I use my flannels at sea, so that one can turn in all standing.[1] The *Lökken* will pay for a new outfit of plain clothes – Summer at last, tho' it has brought down a real blanket of fog. We have a tame Bishop up here: why doesn't our Service Head Priest do something in that line? The Chaplain of the Fleet? He must be a rum sort of bloke, for he has steadily avoided his Peoples Fleet ever since mobilisation. I dined out last night: very seldom that comes off – and, my word, there is trouble brewing. There always has been a good strong under current of friction between, let us say, the Shifter's[2] brigade and the people we work with: that has been very clear to me ever since we started our six monthly visits to the 'Braylock' district, but from what I heard last night .. it's doubled and trebled now. great pity – I'm glad Asquith has given way: just as well he did, over his enquiry into the Gallipoli business and that botched business at Basra. Also, am I glad the Government published those reports from Maxwell to French about Ireland. We want a little common-sense let into this political hot air atmosphere.

Night-night, my Heart. All goes well

Yr: *C*

1. To turn in all standing: to go to bed with your clothes on.
2. 'The Shifter' was the nickname of Captain E.H.F. Heaton-Ellis of HMS *Inflexible* in the Third Battle Cruiser Squadron at Jutland.

A Poster for the *Belgian Canal Boat Fund*. The early defeat of Belgium (August-October 1914) and German demands that Belgians fund the occupation army left people starving. Children suffered most. *(Imperial War Museum PST 2708)*

34. *Monday 24 July 1916*

Sweetheart. Welcome.
May you have a happy and
restful two months in that
very nice and comfy house
– I think of you and the
chicks settled in and wish
you the best of weather.
We are still befogged and
on the cold side, but
'twon't last for always, so
one mustn't grumble. I
shall try and get a good
tramp tomorrow: we are
out on the North Shore –
but can't see it! Good
news this afternoon,
Hindenburg pushed well
back, and the Russians
doing splendidly in the
South. We shall have heavy
losses on our front. The
Germans are quite clearly
all out to hold us – They
are losing more than we
are, and we must set our
teeth and just go on. Here

Belgian Canal Boat Fund
For Relief of the Civil Population behind the firing Lines.
Send them Something.
The Sec. 71 Duke Street
Grosvenor Square, W.

all is very peaceful: we had a real lovely summer evening yesterday: quite
warm. Don't think I have had any letters much and the *Observer* this morning
was simply stodgy. More news from Chatham, the men are all doing well
except that boy Walker – he seems to be hanging fire, I'm afraid – Time is
slipping by: another week and I shall be, what? No statistics! – I asked dear Jaye
Hope t'other night when he was going to be an Admiral – to which he replied
not before next February, but I think he is giving himself too much law – for
he is only four down, and they are almost bound to retire both Luard and
Hunter. Rather a jar when you are made an Admiral and have to give up a big
fat ship: happened up here only t'other day – Well, well. Let us knock off shop
and think of you all in that warm hearted atmosphere: the garden ought to be
looking well if it's a good year for roses – and you'll have the babies playing
lawn-tennis!

Yes, may you all have a very happy time and don't you go barking too much!
Yr: *C*

35. *Wednesday 26 July 1916*

Sweetheart. My word, if you have run into summer as we have, Warblington must be simply 'IT'. I was up very early this morning as we were to have done some running with submarines, but tho' we crawled over from our berth on the other shore (quite a successful sun[n]ing party, and got a lot of sea trout) – we couldn't make our berth and had to drop anchor from 6 to 10 o/c – when it became gorgeous. I have again supped in high circles, and send the card for the Mouse's collection, also some rather nice verses for you, from last week's *Spectator*. My Senator friend, Belcourt had come across a lot of Le M's in Canada, while Mr Bishop, from Newfoundland, also knew a good many – old Peninsular Harry's descendants, probably – Mr McMahon Glynn was Australian, with all an Australian's passion for statistics – The doyen of the party, old man Foster, made a real good speech. Otherwise, my child, all is peace, and everything in the garden is lovely. My new steward, a West Country man, lost his brother at Contalmaison, so I sent him south to square up things: only called up at Easter! Must have volunteered for a regular corps, and got drafted over soon. Saw Roger Keyes[1] this afternoon: he said he had had his name down for a big ship for some time – but *would* have liked a squadron of these ships! There's a rumour that the promotions are to come out tonight, but it's not probable. 'Pon my word, one has almost lost all interest in 'em! It seems C-in-C asked for the regular list to come out, as usual, and then his own, but they wouldn't have it, for some reason, probably Treasury. Glad to say C-in-C is looking much more like himself, he was very under the weather, I thought, t'other day. Night-night, and a good time, and a peaceful one to you.

Yr: *C*

1. Rear-Admiral Roger Keyes attacked Zeebrugge in 1918, succesfully blocking German U boats in port for some time.

36. *Friday 28 July 1916*

Sweetheart: I seem to have come to the 'end of my Latin' as regards writing paper: however, we are so to speak, within the sound of Bow bells – as we arrived in Braylock land[1] only this morning. The usual play. C-in-C says ten days and on arrival one finds that those brigands in the other light squadrons have already made their plans to go up, as well! And what do you think of the promotions? Colin Maclean and Walter Allen I am very glad to see included. I have got one of my men in – Lt. Comdr Manners, But didn't manage Moore – Rather a mistake promoting that Submarine Commander Nasmith[2]. He got a V.C. and promotion from Lieutenant only a year ago. I believe he is 33. Four Admirals are to go, and Luard is just a toss-up whether he has to retire or not – The Admiralty are still worrying me over the *Lökken*. I told the new C-in-C here this morning that 'twas quite clear they couldn't make up their minds, at headquarters, who was the biggest liar – the Master of the steamer or Charles E.! They're going to send a Treasury solicitor along to take evidence.

While I was waiting for a Service motor this morning, I assisted at a most amusing telephone conversation between a supplementary Commander and his landlady, he threatening legal proceedings and the lady, to judge by his muttered very sulphurous comments, telling him to put his head in a bag. Curious comment: War, Service time, 'twas 10. a.m. and this blighter buying a Government line with his private affairs! They are rather that way here, putting their personal business before the state – just like any old dug-out[3] in Kitchener's outfit. I was very amused to find Master Betty (the younger) awful annoyed at Plunkett being promoted! He, Master Betty, has been loafing on shore for nearly two years – Send me a couple of pipes, plain, only they must be lined, for my birthday? [August 2nd] I am down to bed rock, and my last one has just gone back on me – A letter from Hal, speaking more hopefully about Arthur, who is to go on active service, probably Basra way. Night-night, my chick. I have large arrears of sleep to make up as we had it on the thick side last night, and were coming down rather fast. All goes well.   Yr: C

1. This reference is unclear but the reference to old Bruce in Letter 37 indicates that they are at Rosyth; Admiral Bruce was the Superintendent of the Dockyard.
2. Not a mistake. Lt-Cdr Martin Nasmith invented the IS-WAS system of range-finding.
3. Dug-out: a person 'dug out' of retirement.

Part of the Fleet at Anchorage at Scapa Flow *c*.1916. *(Orkney Library and Archive)*

37. *Sunday 30 July 1916*

Sweetheart I am off on the bust, so send you a linelet in case I come back too late for mail time – I gather you are safely settled in and much hope you are really giving yourself half a dog's chance? 'Tis good to hear you say the chicks are pleased, and today you will have the small son as well – trains, guns and all!

Had a long tramp with old Bruce yesterday: good thing to keep up the 'entente'. I have designs on Dockyard labour. There's a good story about him: various Lords of the Admiralty came here to discuss the future of the yard: he was invited to place his views before the meeting. In a very loud voice he said 'Gentlemen, remember there is no finality about ___. Our motto is 'Second to none' ' – Nothing more to be said!   Night–night

Yr: C

38. *Tuesday 1 August 1916*

Sweetheart A linelet to wish you a Happy Month. We have been scouring the seas again – such lovely weather, and I am getting ready to tackle my inquisitor from the Treasury about the *Lökken* – but shan't I just have a fat head! So glad the small son is safely housed and that he is in a good skin. I think you will find he is all right. A parcel of 'undies' and hankies arrived yesterday, very *à propos*, and many thanks. Rowland Nugent may be sad, my dear, but John Scott Luard will be simply rabid. I hear the blue pencil has been run thro' his name – A succession of visitors chiefly about nothing, and my *Torquemada* is to hold his quest on board this afternoon. The Admiralty have sent me a copy of the evidence already taken in the Prize Court. I'm quite sure now that the biggest liar is *NOT* Charles E.

Hug 'em all
Yr: C

39. *Friday 3 August 1916*

Sweetheart. Yrs. of 31st/1st. Don't 'ee worry: one pipe will keep me going – and cholera belts, OUT-size, I have enow – It's very nice to read the chicks' letters and to realize they are really happy. A word in your ear. John Green is so impressed with your good qualities as a tenant, that he places all the garden and orchard produce at your disposal: Here, I come in: Johnny Reeves says use a fish-basket, goes thro' the post easier than a hamper, and let Frost pack me a bag of vegetables once a week? I find all these fellows up here do it, and 'twill save the Steward's book: awful thing, please lend me a helping hand? Six pounds? I have not been able to pay private wages this month, we were out in our Mess accounts – Return Shortly – Well, I really think this place produces more BLIGHT than our real home further North.

I will write about the Osborne interview – 'Tis good to hear the boy has still set his heart on it. His writing has improved: I took his letter for one from Nellie-Nell, but you mustn't tell him so! Tomorrow[1] I have to attend the 'anniversary' dinner – That's twice now. I wonder much shall we have a third? Hardly likely, and yet, who knows –

Night-night. Keep your pecker up: Things are really going quite hopefully. Hug 'em all

Yr: C

1. The second anniversary of the outbreak of war.

40. *c/o G.P.O. Saturday 5 August 1916*

Sweetheart: we are once more feeding in our northern frank [fastness], J.R.J. having telegraphed for us to come back to *Erin*:[1] Something may be in the wind, as it was a most unexpected move, and many loving hearts were incommoded. I shall probably see him this morning. I write after a very enormous and very early brekker, not having turned in after we dropped anchor. Had a bit of a dusting, and oh, dear me, how disgraceful it is that the sailors are still sea-sick! In a way I am sorry we have been torn from our southern haunt, as I had worked a good entente with old Bruce and had a whole lot of work in hand. Otherwise no news, and 'tis a lovely fresh day: quite worth while having been on deck since 2 a.m.

Bless you. Yr: C

1. HMS *Erin* (Capt The Hon V.A. Stanley), 2nd Battle Squadron commanded by Vice-Admiral Sir Martyn Jerram, did not fire at all at Jutland.

41. *c/o G.P.O. Monday 7 August 1916*

Sweetheart – A full morning and a long tramp yesterday afternoon caused me to fail in my Sunday letter. I have yrs: of the 4th and here is the boy's report: quite a good one. It remains to be seen how he gets on these last three terms: Xmas, Winter and Easter, 'cos he won't go up before the Selection Board until May '17. It's a pity he is top of 1A – Frederick fairly hits the right nail on the head: the boy is still rather a baby, not a bad thing, my dear. I had much rather have him that way inclined than one of those dreadful precocious young sweeps, sort of board-school productions, all side and no manners. He will develop and is doing well.

The Admiralty have done 4th L.C.S. very well in the way of honours: my list of recommends has gone thro' without a single switch-out. By the way, I am singularly honoured in the new Navy List. The Lieutenant (S) appears as Flag Lieutenant. We are indeed getting on! A very lovely day, both yesterday and today – My walking companion was Ninety Bernard, who is, as you know, rather deaf, so that the Arcadian (Orcadian) glens resounded with our conversation.

So Frost has gone off? Very probably – weeding never did appeal to a professional gardener. No news – and things are very peaceful. 'Twas a great egg getting you to send up my tweed combinations and brown shoes. Much more comfy: to walk in – I have a whole package of correspondence about the *Lökken* to tackle: the lawyers, confound them, must be coining money over her – and now the Norwegian Government has taken up the case.

Night-night, my Heart. All is peace.

Yr: *C*

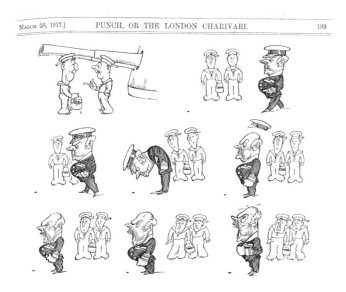

MARCH 28, 1917.]   PUNCH, OR THE LONDON CHARIVARI.   199

'Spit and polish' kept sailors busy. Night-firing practice would have been more useful.

42. *c/o G.P.O. Tuesday 8 August 1916*

Sweetheart. Many thanks your financial assistance and promise of green stuff – albeit Frost has gone off. Finances, my child? Of the simplest. Allotment and Income Tax leave me £25 per month: messing and wages take close on £20 – leaving me a fiver usually devoted to paying outside bills, for one doesn't get thro' much pocket money up here! A peremptory letter from the Bank and from the Stores made me send away £20, and as Admirals will NOT retire, the extra five bob per diem hasn't yet matured. When that comes, I must allot a monthly fiver to Mr Parker on the Hard as my Insurance Premium of £20 is due in October. Don't 'ee worry: we can do it as long as War lasts.

Piping hot here: I have been for a tramp and feel at peace with everybody – even the Prize Court people who are once more at me. I think I told you I had sent in the small son's name? No Service news, somehow. War news quite good. They are wonderful people the Germs: fancy screwing up John Turk to transport heavy guns across the desert? but what beasts they are! This brutal business of rounding up the wretched children of Lille and Roubaix[1] – it is almost inconceivable – and – they will probably give in before we can get into Germany and give them a taste of their own methods.

Rather funny sending Lord Wimborne back to Ireland! Probably Asquith couldn't get anybody else to look at it. Probably Redmond is thankful in his heart of hearts that the proposed so-called settlement wouldn't do? 'Tis something to have it admitted that you cannot coerce Ulster? Did you see that nice little story in the *Spectator* about the old woman, during the height of the fighting in Dublin, trying on a pair of boots from a heap looted from a shop in Sackville Street 'Glory be to God we've got Home Rule at last'!!

Night-night. All goes well and we have the prospect of a little run outside to keep us from getting fat and lazy. Hug'em all

Yr: C

1. The Germans took children as hostages in Belgium and France to force their parents to pay money and food for the army of occupation.

THE "DAMNÈD SPOT."

The Damnèd Spot. (Cartoon by H.M. Bateman from Mr Punch's Navy Pages, March 28, 1917)

43. *c/o G.P.O. Wednesday 8 August 1916*

Sweetheart. Well, my dear, how goes? Up here 'tis real mid-summer, ever so jolly: good weather for scrubbed hammocks, as the old boatswain had it. It was certainly very nice on shore this morning: we have been allotted a small share of the building work going on, and I wanted to see what we were expected to do. Did I tell you I went for a walk yesterday? Not such a very rare event with me now that summer is on – 'twas very jolly, sitting on a clump of heather with one's back to the ships and a clover field quite close – Yes, August and September are *the* months in these parts, and help to make one forget the long dark winter days. Never mind, it will surely be the last winter, and not a 'winter of our dis-content?'.

The Russian news is really excellent. What a nation it is! All depends now on our being able to keep them supplied: I wish our people would realise that, tho' to do them justice, there's not the slacking that there was – we could turn the screw a bit, all the same. We are all very busy boat pulling, good healthy exercise, but I fear me we shall not be able to pull off our Squadron Regatta yet awhile. However, as long as the sailor keeps up the necessary enthusiasm, 'tis all to the good. I was thinkin' only this morning that a grateful country might well have done more for us up here, for 'tis a very large floating population that we have. And now, I turn me with a grunt of disgust to my paper-work.

Night-night. Keep you safe and well.

Yr: *C*

44. *c/o G.P.O. Tuesday 15 August 1916*

Sweetheart: Cheer up – our paper famine is coming to an end as we have at last been able to send our stewards shopping – and the West Country butler from 'a Gentleman's household' who now looks after me in succession to poor Hogan, has been instructed to bring me back a large block with necessary accessories. We got in yesterday after a most interesting trip across to t'other side, having expended our oil to better purpose than we usually do, for we had to see some of our merchant vessels esc(orted): the Baltic, safe across from the attentions of various Fritzes German submarines, lying in wait for them.

Luckily I had a brain wave in the morning, and tubbed at sea, contrary to my usual somewhat loathly habit of deferring soap and water until the anchor is down, for no sooner had we got in than various High Transparencies were at me for news. They seemed pleased, and relieved! But oh dear me, the fog! 'Tis a case of 'Darling I am growing old', for I really did long for my bed last night! We had to rattle thro' portions of it, at times – at pretty high speed. The Admiralty have really done me rather well: I heard yesterday, that they had yielded on the list of four points I was fighting them about, all connected with officers or men. The 'Commends', my dear, are all, I hope, now finally settled. I was told to produce so many names, and, i' faith, 'twas a puzzle rather to fill the bill! For you must always bear in mind that we, of the 'heavies', did mighty little! However, it has been very handsomely settled. I got one direct promotion, three notifications for early promotion, and the names of the four Captains and five senior engineer officers will appear, so *that's* all right. When they are going to publish the Honours List is a mystery.

Yep, the Italians are doing most handsomely – Wonder how long the Austrians will stand the double pounding, and we should be beginning from Saloniki quite soon? All the omens are good.

An eruption of highly placed officers interrupted me just then: owing to the heavy fog the signal that they were coming didn't reach me in time. A cheery lot, all the same. We don't see enough of each other up here, that is one drawback. All goes well and smoothly, while in addition to your green stuff the Guernsey people have sent a large consignment of tomatoes. Can't you picture to yourself my letter of thanks!

Heart up, all is well.

Hug 'em all

Yr: *C*

'Boat pulling', 'good healthy exercise'. Photograph from the Le Mesurier archives.

45. *Thursday 17 August 1916*

Sweetheart: your letter of 13th safe to hand. Here are the Admy requirements for the Osborne entry. Forde will tell you all about the medical part, while you will have the boy's sight tested.

Your enclosure: we *know* now, my dear, why those ships of ours went up: also, do we realise, what very narrow shaves many others had, but nothing has shaken our perfect confidence as to the result should we be so fortunate as to meet them again. As a first-class full dress rehearsal, 31/May/1/June was most useful! – Well, well, let us babble about other things.

The Babies, bless 'em, they shall have a letter. *Tanto*, Anne's birthday approaches. Is she 5 or 6? They grow so fast! Yesterday I had a tramp, so can contemplate with an equal mind the promise of damp rainy weather setting in. News continues quite good. That's a wonderful story, the Munitions Statement in Parliament, and enables one to realise how it was the Huns were able to carry out that big drive last year, East and South East: also, my Word! It makes their having been held up by the French and our wonderful fellows, more wonderful than ever? I wonder, I wonder, whether our stay-at-homes: our many *embusqués*,[1] our chattering useless politicians, our so-called 'Labour Leaders' will they ever realise the debt they owe our fellows over there? Cheer up, my Heart. Have a good peaceful time in that most delightful neighbourhood, and we will yet ramble thro' the Westbourne woods and forget all this nightmare time.

Bless you.

Yr: C

1. An *embusqué* was employed in a non-military capacity at a battle front.

Her father wrote to Alice, enclosing a 'small tip' so that she could buy
a birthday present for her younger sister, Anne. This is the envelope, post marked 22 Aug 16.
Anne's birthday was on the 24th.

46. *Monday 21 August 1916*

Sweetheart. We have been week-ending on the briny – a rather foggy briny, at that, so have been out of touch with the G.P.O. Brother Bosche was rather clever, on this occasion, and scored, distinctly.[1] Hope he will try again! No other news, and all seems to go well. I have received the long promised addition to my family![2] appropriately named when one reads all about the Welsh choir practice. I daren't venture on the name without a dictionary, of last week! How goes the weather with you? Some very welcome green stuff arrived last night in quite good condition. Keep you safe and well: this goes to catch the mail. Am writing the little ones

Yr: C

1. Scheer made a sortie on the week-end of 18/19 August and sunk two light cruisers: HMS *Falmouth* and HMS *Nottingham*. The Navy damaged SS *Westfalen* severely.
2. HMS *Cambrian*.

47. *Monday 21 August 1916*

Sweetheart: You had a very mouldy note this morning, so here goes to make up, for I have polished off my baskets of official correspondence rather more easily than usual. The *Lökken* bobbed up again – the Treasury lawyers wanting more light – Curious, the Norwegian government aren't very well disposed – generally, I mean, while the Swedes, who were inclined, at one time, to be pro-German, are quite helpful. I expect it is because the Germans have been rather high-handed of late, in the Baltic, and have been downing Swedish ships close in, while their submarines don't work very freely outside the Skagerrak. The *Bremen* is a long time over-due – may have been sunk, but it seems the *Deutschland* is safe home again. We are to have a big Fleet boxing tournament tomorrow – it was to have come off last Saturday, only we were otherwise occupied! The arrangements have been made by an old Channel Fleet Commander, and what do you suppose he allotted us, as our share? The construction of the 'Waiting Rooms'!

I have got a copy the small son's birth certificate, and sent it off to the Private Secretary to the First Lord today. Did I tell you Jerry Phillpotts is going there as Naval Secretary? Many thanks, but don't worry about the grey suitings: the interest accumulates – 'tis an ordinary transaction – and I shall now be able to make a regular small allotment to the bank, to pull that lot down, and still, I hope, have a bit in hand to send out here and there. This end of month will see me clear of debt to the Crown. The cake will be very nice: I browse off bread and jam for tea, and a change is welcome.

Had a great brain wave t'other day: the Admiralty have let us take off – I mean up – the blanket coats they issue for cold weather, and I wear mine regularly at sea. Pullar's will dye it dark blue for about ten bob, so I get a quite respectable garment at about a quarter the price of a naval 'British Warm'. The commission, next time you go to Southsea? A new pair of snow shoes, the biggest size made? 9's or 10's. I wear them over tennis shoes at sea, very comfortable, and keep one's feet dry, a tip Colville taught me. Mine have given out after a year's hard work.

Hug 'em all

Yr: C

This boxing tournament on Flotta proved popular for the armed forces serving in Orkney during World War I, judging by the numbers present. The boxing trophies were lost when they went down with *Defence*, but Commodore Le Mesurier replaced one of them.

48. *Wednesday 23 August 1916*

Sweetheart. Here you are, you see, the letter on your writing paper and the Little Mary bulges with cake! Both V.G.I. – The papers will have told you what we were about last week-end: Two light cruisers versus one big battleship, for if they *did* manage to get her back she will be pretty groggy for some time. They were well served by their Zeps and their submarines were much more enterprising than hitherto – 'Tis rather 'Puss in the Corner': if we go over to pay them a visit we have to look out for their torpedo craft – on the water and under the water, if they adventure towards our coast. 'tis the same thing – we have had a couple of good days, tho' yesterday rather cold, and I have actually landed twice running.

The Boxing was quite a show: must have been over ten thousand spectators. All the cups went down in *Defence*.[1] Poor Robert Arbuthnot had got 'em all on board, so the winners got medals instead, one of our sailors got into the final for his weight.

Lemme see, what's the news? I looked at a whole lot of gardens on one of the many islands here: a good few big ships took up gardening for exercise, a difficult job in this very peaty soil, water-logged, at that. George Baird has done quite well – lots of vegetables and a good show of flowers. I hear two admirals have gone – Inglefield and Coke – so that will clear the air a bit. Luard remains on, but retired. I wonder whether all this talky-talk about education will affect Osborne? Ewing – Director Naval Education – and a misfit at that, has been made Rector of Aberdeen or Edinboro' University, so we hope we are rid of him. He was a friend of Jacky's. Talking of J.F., I wonder if the Dardanelles Commission will get his evidence? – There'll be some real scrapping if they do! but we must beat the Bosche before we start quarrelling over our many mistakes. Night-night, my Heart. All goes well.

Yr: C

1. *Defence*, the flagship of Rear-Admiral Sir Robert Arbuthnot in the 1st Cruiser Squadron.

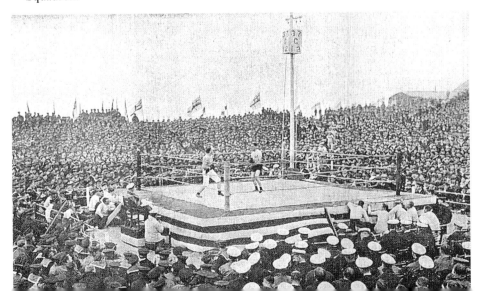

49. *Thursday 24 August 1916*

Sweetheart. We are getting on? Anne is six today and our eldest is applying for Osborne! However, I don't feel so beastly old, for we are on the North Shore once again, and I have had quite a good tramp up a hill. There are objections to these parts as a permanent residence, but no one can deny that the air is good – and, in summer, that the climate isn't ditto. I have your letter of 20th: and have a sort of idea that Hugh Pigott Williams has either retired or gone R.N.R.? Probably retired only, as he's not a very energetic sort.

Everything here seems very quiet, tho' it doesn't follow 'twill remain so, now that they have got their ships repaired: that sortie last week was a most complete surprise, and until we actually got the signal to move off, I didn't believe we were really going.

Looks as if we were moving Northwards from Saloniki? Must say I have [no] use whatever for the Greeks: Constantine or his people, and would much like to see Greece well carved up when all this battery is over. They are dabbling in pretty dirty work too, supplying submarines (as are the Spaniards) and running stuff for Germany. *Tanto* – the Norwegians are much the same! I suppose until we show the world we really are Top Dog, these small neutrals will go on backing and filling? So 'tis all a question of pushing on. Winston Churchill doesn't seem to have made a good impression in Parliament? My Hat! There are some lost opportunities! Well, well. Night-night now. How did my precious Anne's birthday go off?   All goes well.   Take care of yourself Yr *C*

SNOOKER POOL AFLOAT
Commander (as the black he has tried to pot threatens to touch the port cushion).
'LIST HER TO STARBOARD!' (Cartoon by F.H. Townsend, from Mr Punch's Navy Pages, March 28, 1917)

50. *Friday 25 August 1916*

Sweetheart. I don't know my scarlet self! for I have again climbed to the top of a near-by hill, much to my benefit. 'Tis good walking weather just now, with the inhabitants laying in the winter store of peat. Everything seems very quiet. We are to run about early tomorrow morning and then return soberly to berth under the eagle eye of J.R.J., tho' to do the man justice he doesn't worry one over peace trifles. One of the few times, up here, I have realised that we really *are* at War, was when I saw a battleship air bedding on a Sunday!

Talking about Sundays reminds me that the squadron parson wants a mate, in a way he is right, and yet, I don't quite know where to put him. He went away on leave, t'other day, to see the Archdeacon: I hope he hasn't settled the whole thing before I can find a bed-room for the new-comer.

So Parliament is 'up' until 10/October? Rather a relief, for they haven't contributed much to the common weal, of late, and one gets tired of Pemberton Billing, and people of his kidney.

Night-night, my Heart. Keep you safe and well

Yr: *C*

SNOOKER POOL AFLOAT.

Commander (as the black he has tried to pot threatens to touch the port cushion). "LIST HER TO STARBOARD!"

51. *Saturday 26 August 1916*

Sweetheart. Here is a reply to the letter I told you I was writing in answer to Guernsey tomatoes. Who says that Channel Islanders don't stick together?

No news, save that one of my little ships has lost a torpedo, no uncommon thing up here, and in reply to my request for sweeping trawlers I have received an unsympathetic signal to 'utilise the resources of your Squadron' – so there is a 'Sunday misspent' in store for somebody! We ran about and played with various things this morning: had my tub at 5.30, and was relieved to find it still so light, for we are getting on thro' the year?

The hills and vales surrounding this big sheet of water have advantages: yesterday evening, to my great surprise, a picquet-boat from one of the big ships came alongside, containing a shooting party, and disgorged half a dozen brace of grouse, shot that very day! Quite reminded one of old Mediterranean days up the Levant, where, if one had had a good day with the red legs, or woodcock, one dropped a compliment at the bottom of your 'chummy' ship's ladder. I 'spose if ever I get up the Straits again, I may get a chance of letting off my gun again. Those days at Saloniki, when one left the ship at 5.a.m. in the bum-boat, and returned at midnight – Old Mike Seymour's way more the style: out barge with the second anchor and no officers allowed to go ashore until the Admiral had skimmed the cream? Well, well. *Vedremo.* Night-night

Yr: *C*

52. *Monday 28 August 1916*

Sweetheart: Yr: letter 24th and very grieved to hear of the small son's little lapse. Tummy, probably? But he seems to have had a doing. Luckily they pick up easily and 'tis better it should have come out that way, than stay inside? I was regularly demoralised yesterday: lunch at a house[1] some five miles away, then a long walk and taken to tea at a most delightful old house with lots of nice things in it, and scrumptious gardens. And so back on board at 7 o/c with a big basket of roses. Quite an outing. All is very peaceful and we have no news: weather improving, so I still hope we shall make up for our last summer. Our little Padré has come back from leave and I hardly dare look him in the face, as I can't give him an answer as to Padre No: 2, whereas I suspect Padre No: 1 of having brought back No: 2 in his suit-case!

D'you know I had a great find yesterday? rummaging about the Sick Bay? The Inmans sent me up a lot of sevenpennies[2] when we had so many of the men off duty, which were duly sent forward, and I unearthed *The Benefactress*: hadn't read it: already got a new word 'Quatschkopf', something like a 'thick-head' I s'pose? Poor old Hal? I read Maxse occasionally – only very now and then as the *National Review* is rather too strong meat but he gives one new epithets. What do you think of 'Asquithian' as a term of contempt?

There's a lot of banging going on, one of our little ships doing her first shoot, while another little ship goes on looking for a torpedo lost by No.1! Luckily the weather holds.

Night-night. I hope to hear all goes well once more. Yr: *C*

1. Melsetter House, an Arts and Craft mansion on Hoy, where the owners generously entertained officers from the naval base at Longhope.
2. Cheap novels, light reading.

Scapa Flow had access to both the Atlantic Ocean, Ireland and the North Sea, making it a good tactical choice of base, although it was not safe from German submarines.

53. *c/o G.P.O. Tuesday 29 August 1916*

Sweetheart: So cheered at getting better news of the small son, also of the birthday, and that my letters arrived in time. I have yrs: of 24th and 26th. My Dear, you mustn't let Willie Egerton get on your nerves like that! You'll make yourself quite ill, and he isn't worth it! No, no, you have quite enough hay on your fork as it is, so don't go taking in any boarders, albeit your own relations. Say I won't have it!

What do you think of the paper? An extravagance, ordered in a fit of rage when I found the steward had got me a block with envelopes that didn't fit – you remember my old fad? – and before you sent up your purchase. We are all declaring war against Germany now! I am very glad Rumania is in, at last: King Carol, is it? was always a calculator: came in just at the end of the Second Balkan War to down Bulgaria: let's say *Encore* to him now? Besides, 'twill stop a lot of grain stuffs going into Austria and Germany via the Danube – I was on board *Iron Duke* today and heard that Douglas Haig is reported to have told the Cavalry 'they would be employed in their proper role before December'! The old *Spectator* is frightfully bucked about Saloniki – which really looks like maturing into something big –'way back in the dark ages, just after the evacuation of Gallipoli, the *Spectator* advocated making Saloniki a '*Torres Vedras*', criticised by Garvin in the *Observer* as not only arm-chair strategy, but 'grandmother-in-the-arm-chair strategy'. They love each other, these pundits? We are wrangling with the Senior over our annual subscription – 'tis an iniquity that we, up here, should pay full London prices! but I fear me we shan't get much forrarder. Lovely weather, and all goes well. Heart up.

Yr: *C*

54. *c/o G.P.O. Thursday 31 August 1916*

Sweetheart: A Happy Month to all of us! – May September, and October, see good things come about for the Cause. 'Tis a broiling hot day – real summer. We were out and about quite early, doing various quite interesting exercises, and I have just finished a very heavy 'Ship' job. Topping weather, real jam – Very quaint to read in the Marconi news this morning that much annoyance has been caused to the Hun by the amount of German ammunition sent to Rumania. 'Tis really comical! Krupp's working overtime to supply a now declared enemy of the Fatherland.

I had a lengthy sitting in the flag-ship yesterday afternoon – subject Savings Banks for the Sailor. He has no facilities now for saving his pay, but the distrust of his officer is as marked as ever. We little ships say excellent idea but we haven't got the staff: to which the big ship replies 'Work longer hours!' So simple? Wish the horny-handed could be treated in the same way. Not a bad number of the stuffy old United Service Institute Journal this quarter: 'tis a pity the Admiralty have suppressed, pro: tem: our Service *Hot Air Magazine*, the *Navy Journal*,[1] it afforded a very good outlet for these young men to air their views, and gave one quite a good insight into our many side-shows. Night-night, my Heart. All goes well. Yr: *C*

1. The *Naval Review* was suppressed in 1915 for security reasons.

HMS *Iron Duke*, a British super-dreadnought completed in 1914 and named after the Duke of Wellington, was Admiral Sir John Jellicoe's flagship as C.-in-C. of the Grand Fleet until November 1916 when he became First Sea Lord. *Iron Duke* fought at Jutland together with her sister ships *Benbow* and the *Emperor of India*. The fourth ship of this class, HMS *Marlborough* was hit by a torpedo, but repaired to continue wartime service. These huge ships displaced over 30,000 tons, were the first to be equipped with anti-aircraft guns and all survived the Great War. Later, *Iron Duke* became a gunnery training ship and then a depot ship in Scapa Flow in World War II. *(Orkney Library and Archive)*

55. *c/o G.P.O. Friday 1 September 1916*

Sweetheart: Again a 'Happy Month'. I have yrs: of 28th: I *like* your small beer! Quite understand the Mouse's indignation, but that is what is at the bottom of Frederick's[1] cryptic utterances about 'Responsibility'. He doesn't make the top boy 'Head' which is rather a good thing: 'tis an old old bit of school discipline. I think he would like our young Hopeful to be a 'Gang-Boss' but that is his, Frederick's, pigeon. Osborne, plus Dartmouth, plus Gun-room, will soon develop character. I am glad he does something with his hands, for that's an occupation he will find any amount of material at his disposal: the 'shops' at Osborne were filled out on a most lavish scale. There's a lot of engineering enthusiasm engendered there, but it falls away when the boys go to sea and keep watch below!

News is still good. Hindenburg may try a drive at Rumania, but 'tis hard to see where he can get the men and munitions? Something he must do, or he will have the railway cut, and that's a big blow –The map of Europe is much better study now! – Naval news none: those Admirals won't go, it seems. Perhaps the long deferred Honours gazette will get a move on 'em – I had letters from relatives of men we lost. The machinery for adjusting accounts and forwarding private property is lamentably cumbersome. Some of the pension cases quoted in the Press are rather ugly reading, e.g. the man who lost a leg *and* an arm, and had his pension halved in consequence!

Night-night, my Heart. Hug 'em all

Yr: *C*

1. Frederick: Ted Le M's Headmaster at The Wells House School, Malvern, Wells.

56. *c/o G.P.O. Monday 4 September 1916*

Sweetheart: I censor my letters, pro tem, not because my inconvenient sense of duty and example has left me but because I am no longer in my beloved *Calliope*, the pride of the ocean having gone South for her six monthly docking – and I don't see the use of setting a good example to a lot of strangers! 'Tis more comfy this time, as I have worked an exchange: last time, after the boiler room fire, I had to double-back, and that was rather the Deuce and all – We have moved too. A Zep brought down at last! and things moving in Greece – we are getting on! I see Heaton-Ellis' elder boy, David, is wounded? Hope not bad. Tino [King Constantine of Greece] must be in rather a bad way, the Allied Fleet bagging ships under his very nose, his country upside down. Bulgarians in Kavalla and the beginning of a first class fight on his frontiers supported from his own coast-line! A pretty kettle of fish, and no error. Serves him jolly well right, he has been asking for trouble this last eighteen months.

Good weather, at last. Hope the same with you, tho' the evenings must be drawing in, and that ground-mist rising now. A nice part of the country, but too flat? When we settle down, my child, it shall be on a slope. Malvern Hills, eh? But Warblington is a dear spot, all the same.

My locum in *Calliope* got married t'other day – that's why I am occupying his cabins – and has left me a whole pile of light literature. *Honeymoon Dialogues* is one – No doubt about it, English is too heavy a language to go skating over thin ice with. When one thinks of Paulette and her Joseph – the difference! Naval news none: all very stagnant. I see Ryan is leaving Portland, albeit he retired, so is to hang on to the billet. *On dit, on dit*, that he is rather forgetting Mrs Ryan, in a mental home, poor woman, but gossip is always rather unkind. Keep your heart up, my chick, all the omens are good. Hug 'em all   Yr: *C*

General rationing was introduced in Britain in June 1918. *(Imperial War Museum PST 4470)*

57. *c/o G.P.O. Tuesday 5 September 1916*

Sweetheart: You will send my letter on to May? Poor old Hal – only in his last letter he spoke of his anxiety for Lem: and now the boy has gone. 'The last full measure of devotion'. I am rather fond of that Gettysburg speech – a fine end, tho' over young to pay the full penalty. No news here: we are all at short notice, but it may only be a 'buzz' Papers are quite good reading: I only hope the Rumanians are not pushing on too quick – I wonder what Papa Hindenburg thought of the Western front? and now 'tis practically assured we shall bring the Greeks in. I have had a letter from that Le Mesurier boy – Grenville- from Cornwall: he has seen the Sneyds (spelt SNEEDES!) and tells me he goes back to Plymouth College next week, so I suppose our young hopeful will be on his way to Malvern during the next fortnight. 'Tis nice to hear you find him more considerate, as he grows older – good sign.

How is the weather treating you, your last weeks at Warblington? and has the Mouse liked having her pal with her. Perhaps next summer. I think a few days in the country, in flannels, would suit me very well! but we must put the Huns in the back-ground first. I saw a man t'other day who had had letters from a sister of his at *Chateau d'Oix* – and the stories she had heard from our wounded officers and men of their treatment by the Germans! Never again, is what we must teach ourselves to say and, act up to. 'Tis rather a relief Parliament being up – and we seem to get on very well without them. This new Loan must be giving the Germs: a certain amount of *pensieri*: they seem to be beating the financial drum a tidy bit more than usual. Dirty beasts. Night-night, my Heart. Hug 'em all

Yr: *C*

"AND THE LAST THING MY MISSUS SAID TO ME WAS, 'BRING US 'OME SOME SORT OF AN OLD CURIOSITY FROM FURREN PARTS.'"

58. *c/o G.P.O. Wednesday 6 September 1916*

Sweetheart: A rather grey day and a trifle on the dull side. However, the embargo on our shore-going has been removed, so one can get exercise. Good bit of work that youngster in the R.F.C. 'Per ardua ad astra' with a vengeance. One can only hope he won't go and throw his life away, trick-flying, like Warneford. I am sloping disgracefully: we ought to be outside on patrol, but this junk, which has just done her six-monthly docking, was left so full of holes and jobs half done, that I have had to get a gang two dozen strong, of outside workmen, and very lucky to get hold of them at all, to finish her off. As they do NOT go to sea, we sit at anchor and let another take our turn. Practical, if rather lazy. Just now I dream of Defect Lists! Luckily I had a slight acquaintance with them under old Cotton Wool, both East Indies and Channel, so have got some sense of proportion, which is a jolly sight more than some of my Captains have! but our wants are growing, and it is all one can do to get the various items: attended to in the few days allowed. By the way, I don't know if it's true, that the last time the Germs: came out – 19/August 'tis said they only brought out two battle-cruisers, whereas they should have *Hindenburg, Moltke, Salamis* [?][1] *Von der Tann* and possibly one other? – *Lutzow* we know of: also *Seydlitz* said to be sunk in the Elbe. Well, well, time enough to worry about details when it's all over? I have been thinking a lot about that poor boy and rather wondering how May will take it.

I have been watching string after string of Dutch fishing boats being towed out to sea, after a fairly long detention in our harbours. I suppose we have some solid guarantee they won't sell to Germany again? Did I tell you how the official list of 'Captures' vilifies me by saying that '*LÖKKEN*' was seized by a man of war 2¼ miles from the Norwegian coast! An insult, what?

Night-night   Yr: C

1. Probably SS *Derfflinger*.

'And the last thing my missus said to me was, "Bring us 'ome some sort of an old curiosity from furren parts." ' Rescuing sailors from the briny – irrepressible navy humour. Morale was high even in the face of sinkings and drownings. (Cartoon by W. Bird, pseudonym of Jack Butler Yeats, brother of the poet, from Mr Punch's Navy Pages, March 28, 1917)

59. *c/o G.P.O. Thursday 7 September 1916*

Sweetheart: My letters will have told you I had seen that poor boy's name in the Casualty returns? And last night I got yr: letter, and one from the small son and one from Lou, all forwarded on from *Calliope*. Poor Hal: poor May. I much hope she will go out to Cuttack this cold weather. The oculist's [sic] report is a great relief: that's all right? And many thanks for cake, sundries and the snow-shoes – I shall be able to keep my feet dry at sea. News still is good. Nothing much doing afloat. We had a big pow-wow this morning and I was taken for quite a good tramp this afternoon.

Am looking forward very much to the new Navy List, the August copy hasn't got the changes due to the promotions. Ought to get it in a day or two now. Very glad to hear from the small son, and will answer fairly soon. Saw such a very scrumptious garden today – wonder why it is that Scots gardens are such a blaze of colour in August and September, for that's rather a slack month down South? Roses still in full vigour, with sweet peas in full bloom. Trees are just beginning to show signs of turning colour, tho' no leaves off yet. Here comes my evening meal of paper-work, so must shut up. All goes well and smoothly, while the omens remain favourable. Night-night. Bless you

Yr: C

The Assistant Private Secretary writes that the small son's name has been noted and that all is in order.

60. *c/o G.P.O. Friday 8 September 1916*

Sweetheart: Yours of the 1st in last night. I'm glad the small son will have that treat: the modern boy is far more used to motoring than his parents! David Heaton-Ellis – slight wound, back of neck: in a nursing home in town – Padré No: 1 came back from leave t'other day, spent in Wiltshire, and said the wounded seemed pouring in: so I expect our hospital accommodation is rather heavily taxed. The arrangements in France are so good that those ugly stories from Basra seem almost like reading the Crimea over again! Did you notice the announcement of a Colonel Elkington being reinstated? 'Twas he, I think, and another C.O. who surrendered to the Germans during the retreat from Mons, in those long ago early days, and were cashiered. Good fellow that! Hindenburg has all his work cut out for him: 'tis rather significant the hints allowed to creep out in the German Press not to allow of wild wild hopes that all is going to smooth out serenely because Hindenburg has taken over. He seems a bull-headed sort of character, well served by good local knowledge and, at the time he made his great thrust, an ill-equipped antagonist. Whether he can stave off the evil day remains to be seen – September, October, November, about $2\frac{1}{2}$ months fighting weather left – not long enough.

Many thanks, but I am really very well prepared for the winter: can't say I look forward to another spell of short dark days, but it's healthy enough, and the time passes, somehow. It ought to be the last? So let us take heart. Haven't got my coat back from Pullar, but expect it is on the way.

Night-night. All goes well and smoothly   Yr: *C*

'Lem', Havilland Le Mesurier, was the son of C.E. Le Mesurier's eldest brother, Hal. An officer in the King's Royal Rifle Force, he was wounded in France, invalided out then returned to the front and killed second time round (see p. 109).

61. *c/o G.P.O. Monday 11 September 1916*

Sweetheart: I treated you full scurvily yesterday, for a Sunday, but as a matter of fact we used the day to return to our Northern home, where we arrived at 4.a.m. Very lovely night, practically full moon, and a Mediterranean calm sea, but one would have preferred dirtier weather, as submarine reports kept me on the bridge all night, and the ships spread. Don't know what I shall do when my turn comes for a dull old Super-Dreadnought, with comparatively low speed! Taking to a growler after a taxi? John Green came over to wish us well: chiefly, I think to express his admiration of you as a tenant! and so did others: I wonder why? I have yours of 4th: Poor Lulu and Flo. Comes home a bit. Here is the small son's effusion back: he is evidently having a good time. Otherwise no news. I may hear a tit-bit when I go over to report myself. That is good news from Halise – or however it's spelt. 'Tis a big railway junction and once dislodged, the Austrians will find it hard to hold on to Limberg. There was a very interesting *Times* article on why Falkenhayn had to go: it seems he advocated a general retirement, to shorten the line all round, and that he was indignantly over-ruled, as German public opinion wasn't considered sufficiently prepared? May be true: 'tis quite possible. Meanwhile, let us hope they *won't* shorten the line, all the better for our side.

I am in treaty for a second-hand edition of *Consulat et Empire* to read this winter. Do my History a lot of good, and the dear knows one has time enough, those long dark days!

Bye-bye. Keep you safe and well.

Yr: *C*

62. *c/o G.P.O. Monday 11 September 1916 (I find it is Tuesday 12)*

Sweetheart Yrs: of 6th – Give Hal and Flo time, poor people! and then they will, I know, be very proud – very proud. Well, well. Wilhelm has a lot to answer for. Today we have a strong N.W. wind, healthy enough and a trifle on the cold side – I wonder if the boy saw Burton's store at Falmouth? curios from all parts of the world bought from the crews of the sailing ships putting in at Falmouth for orders where to discharge cargo. I haven't been there since *Hecla* days in '91 – Falmouth is now headquarters of the outer Channel trawler patrol Service with old John Denison in charge. No news, or very little. There is a fate attached to that Quebec bridge – the first attempt collapsed about five years ago, very heavy toll of life: some American firm, I think – Smyth, who went to Quebec for the centenary pageant says it's a very wide span to cover, with no convenient island, half way across, like there is in the Forth Bridge, for your centre tower.

They are taking their time aren't they, over the Honours Gazette for that 31/May? I much hope for a D.S.O. for Bickford: fear me he won't rejoin us, as his knee is still very stiff. Fellow I want to push is the Surgeon RNVR, a bounder from Manchester. By the way, Colonel Prentice, father of that boy who was at the Wells House, is now in command of a brigade of 'Churchill's victims' who have been taken over by the Army. I met Edward Gully, now a Lieutenant RNVR on board the flagship yesterday: he told me that the Dardanelles Committee were going to have Winston in the witness box this week! Night-night, my Heart, all goes well and smoothly.

Yr: C

Sailors dropping depth charges to destroy under-water peril. After Jutland, both fleets' tactics shifted to submarine and mine warfare. Neither side wished to risk 'losing the war in an afternoon' as would happen if their navy were destroyed. Germany's unrestricted submarine warfare nearly brought Britain to her knees in 1917, but also starved her own people. *(Imperial War Museum Q18853)*

63. *c/o G.P.O. Thursday 14 September 1916*

Sweetheart – Yrs: of 10th I am *very* glad poor old Hal is coming home to take May back with him, for the winter. I saw that sheep grieve today, who told me his children had been out to see our small ones. He said Southsea had been very hot – made me long for a Southern climate, as yesterday we had our first taste of winter. My word, it was cold! We were running about playing with things – with hail squalls every five minutes just to buck us up. No, my dear, we had better stick to Southsea and freedom of movement. The Mouse? Stick to Norbery and try and get hold of Miss Watson. I don't think the pick of Harley Street could do more. The child is well and vigorous. Knitting up the damaged nerve centres little by little. Faith, patience, and massage – but 'tis hard on you.

I send you a newspaper cutting someone gave me this morning: it reads like *Morning Post*. If the papers would only leave us alone! That reminds me that I saw old Lawson[1] the other day – you may have noticed that his ship got a tremendous hammering? I hadn't realised, until he told me, how short a time they had been in commission. Seventeen days from leaving the builders' yard on the West Coast to putting in for repairs on the East coast! Really our personnel is wonderful – No news up here – Admiral Lowry, they say, has been asked to retire, Richard Poore and Archibald Milne refuse. There will be some fun next Spring, when a vacancy occurs for Admiral of the Fleet.

Night-night Wind gone and better weather

Yr: *C*

1. Captain R.N. Lawson commanded the light cruiser HMS *Chester* at Jutland.

Fond Teuton Parent (to super-tar home on leave). 'And you like your ship, Fritz?'
Fritz. 'I love her! She's a wonder! Such speed! Whenever we race back to port she's been first every time.' (Cartoon by Frank Reynolds, Mr Punch's Navy Pages, March 28, 1917)

64. *c/o G.P.O. Friday 15 September 1916*

Sweetheart: yrs: of 8th – yep, my dear, we were south for a week, our last stay there having been interrupted by a 'STUNT' that after all, didn't mature – Must say, tho' 'tis very flattering that J.R.J. brings us North, so as to have us in our proper place when the Armada puts forth. I should like to have a chance of working under Beatty: different job, entirely – like the advertisement of Portsmouth Ales, J.R.J. 'Will have it in front of him', and what we do is not cruiser work, tho' if all the tales I hear are true, we may yet find the six little ships right in front.[1]

Mrs Hogan's letter gave me the impression that she was very poor, with a large family. Hogan's kit, plus wages and money in hand, realised thirty pounds odd – probably the priest will collar half? Anyhow, you can but try? for it must be a hard job to clothe a lot of young children, and the cold weather is coming on. I shall hear more from Chatham when I get in board *Calliope* next Tuesday or Wednesday, but my last hospital report was quite a good one, young Walker and all.

Glad the small son had a good time – nice trip – cheer up, my chick. Next March, if all goes well, when *Calliope* is due to dock again I will ask J.R.J. to let me go down. All will be well once we have outed the Hun. Meantime the omens are quite good.

Night-night

Yr: *C*

1. Possibly a reference to J.R.J.'s deployment of the 4th Light Cruiser Squadron as lookouts for submarines and mines instead of in its proper role, scouting well forward.

MARCH 28, 1917.]   PUNCH, OR THE LONDON CHARIVARI.   .209

Fond Teuton Parent (to super-tar home on leave). "AND YOU LIKE YOUR SHIP, FRITZ?"

Fritz. "I LOVE HER! SHE'S A WONDER! SUCH SPEED! WHENEVER WE RACE BACK TO PORT SHE'S BEEN FIRST EVERY TIME."

65. *c/o G.P.O. Saturday 16 September 1916*

Sweetheart: Most amazing news in the summary, signalled this morning, of the Press headings for the morning papers – that Greece has sent 25,000 men to fight *FOR* Germany? – Seems almost incredible? if true, 'tis good-bye to TINO, who has been asking for trouble for nearly two years. Apparently the Naval Honours gazette is out – at last! – for J.R.J. gets the O.M. and Beatty a G.C.B. The War news is very good, quite promising. We have been running about this afternoon: real lovely weather to begin with and then rain and mist. We are at short notice today and tomorrow: must say I don't want to go to sea tonight for I have twenty dockyard mateys on board, putting in an anti-Zep gun not taken in hand during the recent refit, and the upper deck is rather cluttered up. Otherwise all seems fairly peaceful. Burney a g.c.m.g. – He was in a very queer frame of mind when I saw him t'other day 'bout one of my little ships, due to go south for docking. J.R.J. turns over all those questions to Halsey, who runs personnel and *matériel*[1] extremely well: Burney, on the other hand, insists on doing it all himself, and it's the deuce and all in consequence. Took me five minutes to fix up *Calliope*, and over half an hour her successor! Funny what a hide-bound set we are – never will de-centralise. I remember Ryan telling me, when he was chief-of-staff to Burney in *Lord Nelson* that the Vice Admiral wouldn't even let him make a leave signal! *On dit, on dit*, that Bacon goes Director of Air Services – Vaughan Lee having let his tongue run away with him.

Night–night. Time's up. Bless you. Yr: *C*

1. *Matériel* = equipment. French words such as *communiqué*, *embusqué* and *matériel* entered the British military vocabulary as the British army was fighting in France.

Admiral Sir John Jellicoe, First Sea Lord, December 1916–December 1917, after a painting by Sir Arthur Cope.

66. *c/o G.P.O. Sunday 17 September 1916*

Sweetheart: Well, my chick, do you want me to sing my 'Nunc Dimittis' and come on shore? now that I have got what you know has been my longing? D'you remember the early days at Portofino, where I told you I wanted *one* thing, to command my own ship? And having got my own ship, I wanted but one thing more, and now it's come? – My dear, I shall cock no end of a chest, with the Legion of Honour to give tone to the Persian Gulf medal, and a C.B. to keep the War Medal company. We really *will* go and be photographed? Don't quite know what to think of it all: had a sort of idea that something of the sort was bound to happen, after Jellicoe came on board and addressed the officers and ship's company, and yet? The list is too impossibly large, and the Battle Fleet rather figure too much, at the expense of Beatty's ships, who bore the real brunt of the fight: What I really *am* delighted at is the Staff Surgeon's D.S.O. Bickford was really admirable. One of our P.O.'s, Willis, a young man I am running for Mate, gets a medal for Conspicuous Gallantry: he was slightly wounded by one of the things that hit us, and he and another man, only two left out of eight, got their gun going again. Four other medals and two mentions, so *Calliope* does well on the transaction. Here is the ship's telegram – ZOATL meaning *Calliope*: 'twas the first intimation I had, as the papers were rather late last night – and I didn't read 'em until I was snug in bed – and, my dear, a high expression of my esteem and regard, dreamt of you! I have yours of 13th, and am very cheered to think you will see Mrs Tate. My very warm salute to her. News is VERY good, quite heart-warming. It's the steady advance that is so cheering. Here nothing. Blowing a gale from N.W. – and I am answering signals of congrats: every ten minutes. The 'Flag Lieutenant' hasn't been so busy for a long time. My little *Calliope* should be coming back in another couple of days. Push on the good work for the trawler people – one cannot have too many neck wraps and mitts: I hope the Italians are better off this winter: there was a shortage of woollen things last year. Night-night my Heart of Hearts. I am very pleased for your sake. Hug 'em all.

Yr: C

Enc: POST OFFICE TELEGRAPHS   Stamped Sept 16 16
FLEET POST OFFICE KIRKWALL

Office of Origin
      Welland
To Commodore Le Mesurier
        H.M.S. Caroline c/o Cyclops
Aberdeen
Heartiest congratulations from officers and ships company
ZOATL

67. *c/o G.P.O. Monday 18 September 1916*

Sweetheart: How goes? After blowing a hard gale from N.W. all yesterday, it's now backed to N.E., harder than ever. Two anchors down and steam up, quite in the old winter way. Here are Ronald Hopwood's verses from the *Times*. Someone told me that Hopwood, when offered a Dreadnought up here, declined 'as he couldn't stand the strain' – which was honest of him? so he is an Admiralty stool polisher. But, my dear, my dear, if those Admiralty *embusqué*'s are going to have any share of the plunder going when we have settled accounts with Wilhelm, what about those at sea? Can you wonder that there is a tinge of jealousy leavening the service? However, Padré No: 1 gave us a clinking good sermon on: 'A little leaven leaveneth the whole lump', and as Charles E's thank-you, is in the boat 'shore-off'!

A long letter from *Calliope* setting out progress made: I hope she is on her way back. Very good news again this morning, a thousand yard gain near Thiepval: we are certain to have Combles soon, and the French Peronne. These new armoured cars[1] must be disconcerting things: an armoured box with three machine guns on a motor lorry chassis, the wheels shot with flat metal plates like what is known as a 'caterpillar tractor', short of a direct hit from a gun, they are fairly fool-proof.

When do you have to go back to Southsea? The chicks will be very mournful, I'm afraid, and 'tis a nice country all round, with nice warm-hearted people – The *Vernon* people threaten me with a further series of torpedo trials, but *Calliope* has acquired such an unsavoury reputation for breaking up her mountings that some other ship is to do them. The torpedo department of the Service has not come out too well.

Night-night
Yr: C

1. The first tanks.

Muirhead Bone, R.A. *Tanks*. Commodore Le Mesurier said they originated with the Admiralty. (Letter 71) They helped soldiers on the Somme but were fatal to their crews if they received a direct hit and fire broke out inside. *(Imperial War Museum 1341)*

68. *c/o G.P.O. Tuesday 19 September 1916*

Sweetheart: *Evviva moi!* indeed – and so you are pleased? Well done. I went to wait on J.R.J. this morning, to thank, and he said very nice things: you see the big ships, without a secondary armament of six inch guns, rely very much on my little push to keep off the German destroyers, which we had the good fortune to be able to do. *Personally* I attach much more value to the torpedo, and tho' J.R.J. gave me a wigging for having pushed in, that evening, to easy torpedo range, I am convinced it was right.

I have a telegram that my precious *Calliope* leaves this afternoon, so hope to be on board the lugger by noon tomorrow. We have had a blowy 48 hours, but 'tis rather less wintry just now and that is about all the news up here. Papers are quite good reading: it all comes a little too late in the year to get the full value, but 'tis all in the right direction. Did I tell you that there has been a row in the Air Service, and that Vaughan Lee is to go? His tongue has always got him into hot water, able little fellow as he is. I met a very radiant young man on board the flag-ship this morning, a young post captain who has been at the Admiralty up till now, and has just got a little ship up here. Don't think I have ever seen a man more pleased with life and simply delighted to get away from the Admiralty! That's the way to look at things

Night-night now   Keep you safe and well   I am so glad for your sake.
                                    Yr: *C*

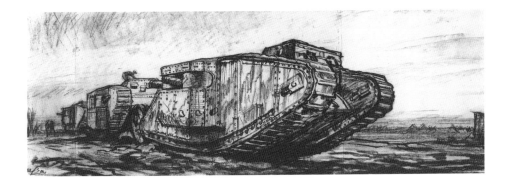

69. *c/o G.P.O. Postmarked 5.30 a.m. Saturday 23 September 1916*

Sweetheart. Once more aboard the lugger and jolly glad to get there after three weeks away. I am wrestling with an awful fat head (we have been out for Manoeuvres) my strong disinclination to do any paper-work. And a pile of letters all to be answered, somehow. Hug the small ones for their very nice and well written notes. My dyed duffel coat has arrived, and looks a most respectable garment: good enough for the bridge, at sea, but hardly good enough to wear in the train when I *do* get any leave!

News sounds all right, and not even little Willy's oak-leaves of the order of merit will serve to hide the failure at Verdun? Heigh-ho. I am very sleepy, and we are out from 8 to 10 p.m. doing some much needed night firing: Almost ashamed to think how much time has lapsed since we last did target practice after dark but then it must be remembered that May/July the nights are very short?

And now I must off.

Bless you all
Yr: C

"Looks to me like a bad case
of food hoarding!"

70. *c/o G.P.O. Saturday 23 September 1916*

Sweetheart. I feel less of an owl after sleeping like a stone dog, tho' what with Night Firing and a very heavy mail I didn't tumble into bed much before midnight, after all. I censor this, to send you one or two letters, besides Paterson's:[1] he must be very fond of our small son? Just as well we happen to be emergency squadron, as I have HEAPS of letters to write. I must now fight the Admiralty over the young P.O. I am running for Mate: some wiseacre up there says he isn't eligible: just like them. My new coat is a great success and looks nice and inconspicuous, while it won't show the dirt! – Tell the boy I have his letter and will answer in good time. I *think* he saw '*REPULSE*': she is up here now. News is all still very good, and Von Mackensen has apparently failed: there was just a chance that he might have repeated his big drive of last year, but I suppose we have all made up lee-way with guns and munitions by now. 'Tis the most cheering sign of the whole lot as is the report that the Germans are using Turkish troops on the RIGA front – Fall back, shorten their lines they must, and that will be the real beginning.

Bye-bye. Bless you all

Yr: *C*

1. Paterson was E.K. Le Mesurier's housemaster at The Wells School.

Postcard sent by the Le Mesurier children's Nannie to her young charges in 1917, when food shortages were at their worst.

71. *c/o G.P.O. Sunday 24 September 1916*

Sweetheart: Such a pefect day and I have had a tramp and feel very peaceful. Poor old Hal: A long letter from Cuttack 28th August: he hadn't heard then – Arthur has gone off to Mesopotamia, 27th Punjab L.I. From what Hal says, the Commission of Enquiry will fairly dance with rage! I am nearly thro' my letters, have rather put off the Service stuff and am expecting to get heartily scrubbed quite soon! Good news today, two Zeps down – Make 'em a bit chary-like.

That was a very good description by the Italian general staff of the kind of fighting they have put up. Allowing for the natural exaggeration of the language, it has all been good work. Very difficult country. These 'Tanks' – I am so cheered they originated at the Admiralty! – seem to put the fear of God into the Hun all right. That's a lovely story of one of 'em picking up a German Colonel out of his trench and carting him about all day, until they had time to send him off to the rear!

Past time. Night-night. Bless you
Yr: *C*

Light Cruisers in line 'The speed of these little ships is their principal safeguard.' (Letter 14) Zig-zagging at top speed of 29.5 knots saved the 4th L.C.S at Jutland. Jellicoe wrote in his Despatches, 'The Squadron was handled with great ability.' *(Imperial War Museum Q18324))*

72. *c/o G.P.O. Monday 25 September 1916*

Sweetheart: Yrs: of 21st and so the small son has gone back to the Wells? 'Twill be rather a critical term: had he not been as he is, one would be thinking of a public school, young as he is. Wasn't his fault, or, the dear knows, ours, that he had to be pushed out so young. However, he is doing well: modest: and if he has not yet got this sense of responsibility Frederick craves to see him develop, 'twill come all right. I have done my extra bit of Service paper-work, brought about by the 'P.Z.'[1] we had t'other day: rather an interesting one, but it comes a bit heavy on the small ship, the mass of returns. I have to take two, perhaps three, officers away from their gun-quarters, to help plot. Was looking today thro' the appointments: my old *Cornwallis* midshipmen are now acting sub-lieutenants – one V.C. and three D.S.C. – not bad for one gun-room? While young Morse got a D.S.O. and the boatswain a D.S.C. – George Hope told me that had John Davidson not been so pig-headed, and done what he was told to, that the losses on the HELLES beach would have been far less. John was ever obstinate. Mortimer L'Estrange Silver has come home and goes to a shore job at Chatham.

Weather still holds good, such a joy – tho' it does seem to encourage the Zeps? Cake has turned up all serene, and is quite a triumph. Yep, we must comb out the Government offices, by Gum, I'd begin on the Admiralty tomorrow! and put some more men in training: we shall want them next year. It's all damn nonsense this army of quill drivers –

Night-night, my chick. All is very peaceful.

Yr: *C*

1. 'P.Z.' Tactical exercises.

73. *c/o G.P.O. Tuesday 26 September 1916*

Sweetheart: Yrs: of 23rd, and so you are really back in our own home? Might be worse – and the small ones have a very good room for a nursery. Nothing doing here, after a somewhat disturbed night – Our notice for steam, i.e. the no: of hours before having the main engines ready to move, began to shorten at midnight – last night. I must tell you that there has been a great 'buzz' up here, that the Second edition of 'The Day' was due 27th/28th – gradually we went to one hour, and then at 7 o/c to ½ hour, so it really looked like business, when came the anti-climax 'As you were'.

Old Tate writes very pleased at having seen you and the boy. The pudding-faced clerk has just come to me with a reference sheet which I told him to draft out to an inspector of Police re a young stoker breaking leave. 'Please Sir am I to put C.B. after your name'. We are getting on? We had an indignation meeting of members of the Senior, this morning, and have asked for a general meeting on the subject of our annual subscription – during War – I doubt anything coming out of it, as we cannot very well be represented. It is rather iniquitous that whereas Boulogne and Havre are 'FOREIGN PARTS' within the meaning of the Club rules, these far more inaccessible Northern fastnesses are United Kingdom and therefore 'Home'. I will cheerfully let ANYONE and EVERYONE, Admiralty officials for choice, have all my share of 'HOME' privileges, up here, once War is over!

Papers simply yelling with joy over the two Zeps: rather admire the IRON CROSS brigade for coming again so soon – you must watch your lighting.

Night-night

Yr: C

Royal Marines pull a slim sailor through a battleship's 15-inch gun in order to clean it. The minimum chest measurement required for naval entry was 32 inches. *(Imperial War Museum Q17961)*

74. *c/o G.P.O. Wednesday 27 September 1916*

Sweetheart . You will all be safely home by now, 5 o/c? and the small ones have got over their grief at leaving Warblington? We shouted with joy at the news this morning THIEPVAL and COMBLES in our hands: 'tis great doings.

I got the captains on board this morning for a pow-wow, and told Martin to rig the black-board: when we came in I found he had pushed the table to one side and had arranged a regular school circle! Talking about school, reminds me that we have, at last, got a Naval School-master in each ship, so now we can go ahead. Interesting career, our man: A.B. Royal Naval Division – just after Antwerp: then a writer, and finally a Naval Schoolmaster, C.P.O. Was assistant science master in a Board School – sort of H.G. Wells' *Love and Mr Lewisham* type – but the fellow I like is an ordinary seaman we have here: enlisted as a driver R.F.A – giving his age as two years more than it was: went over with the first lot, was in the retreat from Mons and the Aisne, bought out by his people as too young – and goes to sea as a Seaman 'Hostilities only'. He was at one of the after 6 inch guns when we were getting that dusting – and later on, was asked by the officer of the quarters which he preferred, Navy or Army? To which he replied he thought Army, as at least you had a 'funk-hole' to drop into! But a good fellow all the same – we could do with more of the same.

All goes well and smoothly. Keep a stout heart

Yr: *C*

75. *c/o G.P.O. Saturday 30 September 1916*

Sweetheart. A Happy Month (and tell the Mouse she is jolly lucky to have such a nice home!) Bless her: one feels all the longing to get away from pavements! And so you have had a Zep at last? Portsmouth has been singularly immune: on the other hand, it is well protected: a whole gang of A.A. gunners, and guns, are always in training at Whale Island, while *Vernon* is well to the front with search lights. I hear indirectly that Weymouth and Portland were warned: if only War goes on long enough, and the Huns display enough energy, we shall wake up Plymouth, still a sleepy hollow.

All very quiet up here. We ran about yesterday afternon, and again until after midnight, and I have had a good long tramp, so all is peace. No letters, but the news continues very good indeed. What wonders our fellows are doing on the Somme! Very critical time for the Germs: just now: they have a bare four days to raise their loan in, and it seems so far, a failure. A very chastened tone in their Press. But, but, we haven't got 'em flat yet, by a long chalk.

Yes, I hope the small son will have a good term and not slack: I *think* his tendency that way has left him? I will write him quite soon.

Keep you safe and well. All is smooth up here.

Yr: *C*

198   PUNCH, OR THE LONDON CHARIVARI.   [MARCH 28, 1917.

ECHOES FROM JUTLAND.

Wine Steward (acting as one of Ammunition Supply Party). "WILL YOU TAKE LYDDITE OR SHRAPNEL, SIR?"

76. *c/o G.P.O. Sunday 1 October 1916*

Sweetheart: Again, a Happy Month: May it be a good one for the good cause. No news, and all is very quiet: I am stuck for a most unpleasant job tomorrow, sitting on a court-martial on two very old personal friends. Beastly business.

I have been reading the published extracts from Bethmann-Hollweg's speech: Not what you would call a very convincing argument? but he takes the opportunity, like a good German – are there ANY good Germans? to dissociate himself from any tender feelings towards England. Too late, I think? but we must be on the look-out for their nasty tricks.

Two things I think we can do, tho' it is 'Reprisals' – and reprisals are rather a two-edged sword – we should tell the German government that for every air-raid over England, an open German town will be bombed, and that for every English prisoner of war maltreated, a German will be punished? The French have done both, with very good results. *Also*, make it quite clear, ton for ton of merchant shipping submarined. We are top-dog now, and should take the high hand. Keep your eye lifting for a first-class row over the next promotion to Admiral of the Fleet: *On dit, on dit*, they want to get P.L.[1] in, to the detriment of Richard Poore and Archie Barkie,[2] tho' the latter is a rotter – and the governing considerations were altered, by an Order in Council, never published, when P.L. was Second, no, First, Sea Lord!

Bye-bye. Hug 'em all

Yr: *C*

1. Prince Louis of Battenburg.
2. Admiral Sir Archibald Berkeley Milne, nicknamed 'the Arch Bark' by his terrified crews.

Wine Steward (acting as one of Ammunition Supply Party). 'Will you take lyddite or shrapnel, Sir?' (Cartoon by F.H. Townsend, Mr Punch's Navy Pages, March 28, 1917)

77. *c/o G.P.O. Monday 2 October 1916*

Sweetheart – So you are settled in? I hope you squeezed the landlord? Very satisfactory to think that Norbery speaks well of the Mouse, and her general condition. It seems to have been a really successful two months?

We had a rumour this morning that yet another Zep had been brought down: they must have got fairly handy to here, as we heard Telefunken Wireless last night and we don't usually get it in these parts – No anti-aircraft gunner can shoot without practice, but I don't think it VERY likely Zeps will make often down the South Coast, as they have to keep pretty high up.

A really lovely day, with a cold snap in the air. We had a great local pow-wow – question of manning, and how many men we can train. No doubt about it, that the material we are now getting to replace men sent South, is not what it was – Can't expect it? The numbers are there: Each depot has an overflow camp, and close on ten thousand men on the books, so there is no shortage. Curious the number of grocers' assistants I come across – Able Seamen (save the mark) 'Hostilities only' – Shouldn't care to commission a big ship now!

All goes well and smoothly. I have sent the small son five bob. Hug 'em all
Yr: *C*

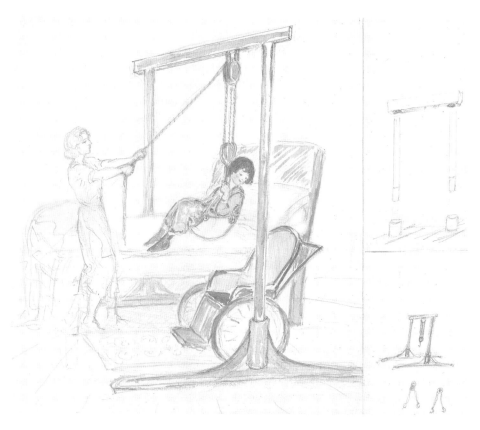

78. *c/o G.P.O. Tuesday 3 October 1916*

Sweetheart, Another Zepp: making four. We are getting on! Wonder what 'Tino is thinking about? if what I read in *The Scotsman* is correct, that the Royal bodyguard at Tetoi are beginning to desert he'd better pack his bag pretty quick. By the way, has this extraordinary rumour reached you, that Lloyd George was put up to give that interview with the Yank, as the German Government had approached ours, thro' a third, neutral party to ARRANGE AN ARMISTICE while they evacuated Belgium! There's a yarn and a half for you!

Third of the month: should get my new Navy List tomorrow: pity one has to burn the old one now, and sign on that it *has* been burnt. Got into an awful stew yesterday – monthly muster of all confidential books and documents, one precious sheet missing – F.O.U.N.D. after much search, in the cabin of the man who was loudest in his protests that he had never seen the document in question. 'Twas ever thus – but it gave me rather a turn. This week bids fair to be on the quiet side: I hope to get out, with five of the six ships, to do some exercises, towards the end of the week. Otherwise, we wait on the Hun. *On dit* that Henry of Prussia has taken over the H.S.F.? What *I* should like to do, would be to catch little Willy bending, at sea, and down him, but I suppose it is too wild an idea that he will ever go afloat? How blood-thirsty one gets, and how very rightly so, when one meditates on those beasts and all the harm they have done. Bethmann-Hollweg's speech has not had *'une bonne presse'* even in his own country. A very chastened tone. So be it, he deserves it all.

Night-night now. All goes well up here

Yr: C

Margaret's legs were of different lengths (Letters, June 30, 1916). She was paralysed from the waist down and had to spend much of her childhood in a bath chair, lying down. Foffs acquired a hoist and wheelchair sketched here by her sister Hetty. Margaret lived in the editor's family home for nearly 20 years. She learned Braille and corresponded with the blind, and made monthly sketchbooks for disabled 'post' Rangers.

Letters to Ted 'the small son' about Jutland

(now in Special Collections, Brotherton Library, University of Leeds, Leeds LS2 9JT).

79. *Saturday 10 June 1916, HMS Calliope*

Dear old man. Mummie will have told you she got my post-card, at last, on Tuesday? We got back here on the Friday, 'bout midday, but I couldn't get into my cabins for a bit as we had some of the badly injured in 'em – so I must have missed the outgoing mail that afternoon. I sent Margaret a lump of stuff that was picked up on the bridge – we had a ricochet burst right thro' there – and got hit aft two or three times as well. The German gunnery was clinking good until our big ships got on to them – when it went off tremendously. The battle-cruisers and the four '*Queen Elizabeths*'[1] did wonderfully well: had a real good hammering and gave as good as they got: our destroyers too - were tophole – much better than the Germans.

My little outfit has been credited with two German destroyers and we claim a fat big battleship as well – though I see other people are on the same lay! while we must have had a good half dozen torpedoes fired at us. Great pity the failing light and thick haze saved 'em. As it was they were badly rattled and deuced glad to get home. One of our destroyers waddled into harbour on the East Coast with a large slab of a German light cruiser hanging on to her bows! How on earth she got home Goodness only knows. No, the Huns will keep quiet at sea for some time: a thousand pities the Admiralty made such asses of themselves as to sing 'Miserere' that Friday night, or evening – We lost a lot of men, I'm afraid: close on a dozen – and had a good many more crumpled up rather badly. Wonderfully cheerful about it all –

Give Frederick and Paterson my love – tell 'em we've got our tails up all right. Chin-chin to Thurston, Napier and Pearson. Buck your cricket up and practice fielding. A good field is nearly always a good bat – Question of eye.

Yr

Dad

1. The 5th Battle Squadron – *Warspite, Barham, Valiant* and *Malaya. Queen Elizabeth* was absent, having a refit.

Muirhead Bone, R.A. *A torpedoed merchantman on the shoals – Salvage officers making a survey.* Stopping food and raw materials going in and out of Germany was a never-ending job for the Navy in the North Sea. But it was still possible to claim prize money. Commodore Le Mesurier took *The Lökken,* a Norwegian iron ore ship and won her as a prize. (*Imperial War Museum 918*)

80. *3 August 1916, HMS Calliope*

Dear old man. Many thanks your letter: you seem to have had quite a good term and to have got well over that rotten finger which gave you so much trouble in March. I am writing about putting your name down for the Osborne entry next year. Don't think we shall have fixed up the Hun by then, though he will be pretty groggy – I ought to get the summer hols: of next year with you all: long time since we had any hols: together?

Don't know there is very much I can tell you about that Jutland business: when 'CALLIOPE' and the others were really in it we were far too busy running away to bother our heads about much else! Our first excursion was like a stage play or summer pageant! Smooth sea, bit misty. German destroyers, about a dozen of 'em, rushing towards us, tho' they didn't come very close. I saw a salvo from *Calliope* land fair and square on one boat and saw her crumple up, while the other ships made some more of 'em pretty sick: then we had to avoid their torpedoes, while the Huns made big smoke clouds and disappeared.

Number two excursion began the same way, tho' those fellows didn't come in as much, and then, all of a sudden, we found ourselves on top of the High Sea Fleet. We could make out seven or eight battleships: Perhaps we hung on a bit too long, but we think we got one torpedo home.

Running back was quite an experience: we had to wag about like a snipe, with the stuff falling pretty thick all round us. That bit I sent Margaret nearly got the Navigator next door to me – 'Tis a great pity we weren't able to really finish 'em off, for they had quite as much as they wanted and a bit more.

Weather is better now, much warmer. I expect you'll get some cricket this time: good place, Warblington. I am very fond of it. The Admiralty are bothering me a good bit about that ship we picked up last May, but I think we have managed it all right. The fellow is trying to bounce for all he is worth. So long, old man. Keep on plugging at it. You're getting a big chap now so look after your Mother – you can help her a good deal.

My love to Margaret and the babies. Take care of yourself and have a good term when you get back.

Your

Dad

81. *8 September 1916, HMS Calliope*

Dear old man. Many thanks your letter and very cheered to hear Mr. Inman was so pleased. Eyes are dicky things and one never knows when they may let you down. Our last outing wasn't much to write home about! And the Huns nearly came off best, for though we bagged a big battleship of theirs she has got home, worse luck, to their getting two of our light cruisers – they deuced nearly got some of our big ships. They were well served by their Zeps, who scouted for them top-hole. One gets a crick in one's neck looking for Zeps: and a positive squint trying to spot submarines –

The answer from the Admiralty about my sending in your name is on it's way – as the Private Secretary tells me it was posted on the 24th.

Very hard on your Uncle and Aunt; GOOD CHAP, Lem: Well, well.

I remember Garnett all right, but not L'Estrange. Mummie tells me you have been swept off for a joy-ride, so have a good time. Give Frederick and Paterson my love when you see them.

Good luck

Yr:

Dad

King George V and Admiral Sir David Beatty, Commander-in-Chief of the Grand Fleet on the flagship HMS *Queen Elizabeth* in June 1917 at Scapa Flow. He is the DB referred to in Le Mesurier's 'last' letters. The King visited the Fleet in order to bestow in person honours earned at Jutland. Commodore Le Mesurier was invested with his CB on 24 June 1917.

Last Letters

82. *Noon Sunday 15 July 1917*

Sweetheart: Back to duty: no verdict yet from the doctors – and nothing from C-in-C – Osmond Brock did not get my letter until yesterday evening – Quite a good journey and I was on board by 9.30. Have just waded thro' my papers – we remain the only L.C. Squadron with the Battle Fleet – and Alan is made an Acting Captain . . .

Such a treat, my Heart, to have seen you all! A very heartsome green patch to look back on – you are, as always, a wonder – Now I must off to pay my official calls.

Bless you all

Yr: C

83. *Monday 16 July 1917*

Sweetheart – I write you in letters of 'ber-lud'[1] as Martin has forgotten to fill my ink pots – and all hands are out on the jetty while the ship is going thro' her stability test. Nothing yet, either from the Doctors or Osmond Brock. I met his lady wife yesterday at the Slayters. Rained yesterday, so got rather wet doing my official calls: slept like a stone dog. The new Navy List puts me number 52 – on the first page. Little Ninety Bernard has been given the vacant A de C: I am hanged if I would run about with my tongue hanging out, were I passed over? Mrs Slayter gave me a most welcome box of eggs – and the steward has laid in large supplies of milk. Ship very upside down, but can't be helped – So Bethmann-Hollweg has gone? Should think he is rather pleased: a very thankless job. Keep you safe and well, my Heart – and a good six weeks summer at Emsworth.

Bless you: Hug the chicks

Yr. C

1. Red ink.

84. Tuesday *17 July 1917*

Sweetheart: My ultimatum has come – hospital treatment for a fortnight or three weeks 'essential' – and C-in-C has let me have three weeks Sick Leave – – which is jolly good of him. We are out in the stream, with the dockyard finishing off – and I expect my relief – as Captain of '*CALLIOPE*' tomorrow.

'*VANGUARD*'[1] incident seems to have been very distressing: some of the officers were away, on board another ship, at a Sing-Song![2] Nothing much seems to have happened during the fortnight on leave and Townsend is quite cheery – No more time.

Bless you all
Yr: C

1. HMS *Vanguard* blew up while at anchor off Flotta, Scapa Flow, in July 1917.
2. A sort of ENSA ship – specially for entertainments.

85. *Wednesday 18 July 1917*

Sweetheart – I have yrs of 15th: Cheer up, my Heart: I firmly believe a fortnight or three weeks will fix up my old tummy . . . David Beatty has wired the Admiralty for a young Captain for '*CALLIOPE*': he sent for Townsend yesterday afternoon – and sent me a very nice message that I wasn't to get rattled and that my job would be kept open. Now I must get into dry dock as soon as I can - Hug the chicks: if they let me out between whiles, I will come hot-foot to Emsworth. Green trees more than London streets! – tho 'tis very nice and dear of the Halls to think of us stopping in Cranley Gardens – We are at short notice, with a rainy day to cheer us up – otherwise no news. Saw Johnny Reeves this morning. Winston back in the Ministry! And Eric Geddes blossomed into First Lord. We move. Keep you safe and well and hug the chicks –

Yr: C

86. *Friday 20 July 1917, United Service Club, Pall Mall SW1*

Sweetheart – Just back from seeing Tripp: I go to hospital 'Officers' Section, Guy's Hospital, London Bridge S.E. now – and shall be a week at least in there – as they want to look at my 'Swallow-pipe' . . . When we know more, we will fix up plans.

Yr: C

87. *Saturday 21 July 1917, Guy's Hospital, SE*

Isn't it great? 'Honourable mention' – only awarded 4 out of a 100![1] Well done our side! Got in here early yesterday, and have made a start: am being kept in bed and on slops pro tem. Quite comfy: A little public – and too many 'Ministering Angels' – Tripp non-committal yesterday – I have plenty of clothes, my chick, so do not bother to send – and get my papers from outside. Hug 'em all – Bless you

Yr: C

1. Reference to Ted Le M's success in the Royal Naval College Osborne entrance exam.

88. *Guy's Hospital, Sunday morning*

Sweetheart. Am still 'all over, like' about the small son's success. Isn't it jolly? And how many years is it that we – and he – have set our respective hearts on getting in? I got your wire very soon after I had seen the paper, and had written the boy a line, as well as a note to both Frederick and Paterson. Well, my dear, I am up and much cleaner after a tub and a shave: a big Ward with cubicles. Very empty and very quiet. Some big throat man is to shove a pipe down my neck on Thursday and as I am distinctly better for the quiet and routine I may as well stop here for this week, anyhow.

Good for old Tyrwhitt: everyone is very pleased – the first Captain to be made a K.C.B. - Sounds like air raid warnings going on – Otherwise no news. Did you see Colin Maclean got a D.S.O.? Cheer up: I am very well looked after. Hug the chicks: tell 'em how pleased I am about Teddy.

Yr: C

HMS *Vanguard*. 'Some of the officers were away, on board another ship, at a sing-song.'

89. *Monday 23 July 1917, Guy's Hospital*

Sweetheart – A whole batch of letters, a parcel and a cap cover. What more could I want? (except a new tummy?). Bless the chicks for their letters, and hug 'em – Anne really very touching! All is quite peaceful – and the Air Warning of early yesterday was for the HARWICH raid. Thursday, my Heart? I am to be 'gassed' that day and have a tube shoved down my throat – so it doesn't sound hopeful? I'll let you know when I hear the result of this exploration.

It is nice about the boy? I am still quite warm through over it and picture to myself Hugh Pigott Williams making faces! Not very Christian – but very human? And so, my chick, transplant the flock to that nice house, and have a spell yourself. I had an Admiralty surgeon, an old friend of mine – to visit me on Saturday – just to satisfy the Department I was not a fraud!

Keep well – Yr: *C*

90. *Tuesday 24 July 1917, Guy's Hospital*

Sweetheart – Had a good move? I rejoice in your flowers, they travelled very well indeed, and yr: letter – Here is a real nice note from Paterson to make your heart swell with pride . . .

Russia? A big query: much depends on what we can do up on our left: some wounded gunner officers in here tell me the Germans have got a lot of guns up and that our batteries are having a bad time. Rather borne out by the Casualty lists…I did hear that J.R.J. had been North to talk to Beatty –

Fare you well, my Heart – and take care of yourself. Hug the chicks. It *is* nice about the small son.

Yr: *C*

Ted Le Mesurier as a young cadet.

91. *Wednesday 25 July 1917, Guy's Hospital*

Sweetheart – How goes? And have you all fitted in well? Hotham[1] came to pay me a visit and I was taken for a drive – but dear me: I don't like the War news – political and military – I had pumped into me . . . The Russian news is worse than ever? Tho', as a set-off, the Crown Prince hasn't shifted the French off that ridge . . . any day now we should have the word as to our move in the West? What do you think of a purely Labour Government at Westminster? I heard it quite openly talked about last night.[2] Lloyd George is seemingly on the down grade.

Here is a letter from Frederick you can tear up – and Townsend writes that all goes well. Have a good time, my chick, and get as much rest as you can – Hug 'em all.

Yr: C

1. A.G. Hotham, Captain of HMS *Comus* in the 4th Light Cruiser Squadron.
2. First Labour government took office in 1924.

92. *Thursday 26 July 1917, Guy's Hospital*

Sweetheart – A linelet, my child, and I will ask the Sister in charge of us to add a word this evening – No news – all is very peaceful and actually, yesterday evening, I got down, and held down, some fish – so we *are* getting on? Don't think me hard hearted: if they want to keep me, you shall come up – Bless you.

Yr: C

93. *Friday 26? July 1917, Guy's Hospital*

Sweetheart: I have been hanging on for the doctor's visit, about tomorrow. Will send a wire, as soon as I find out – Meantime, I am to stop here over Tuesday: Patience, my chick, if so be you do come to London Bridge – the station is but one street from the hospital: visiting hours 3–6 – I got up early this morning, to tub, but realised I was a bit of a crock, and so to bed again. Doctor just been, my child, and I shall not be fit for publication – but heart up, for early next week I hope to be with you.

Bless you.
Yr: C
Emsworth 27 July 17

Enc: P.O. TELEGRAPH: 'very sorry tomorrow off writing'
Lemesurier

94. *Saturday evening, 28 July 1917, Guy's Hospital*

Sweetheart: A pathetic note, my poor lamb, about your last letter and your Wire: Cheer up, my Heart. All is really going well – Tripp has gone North, he is one of the recognised consultants to the Fleet, so I shall not hear the result of that exploration last Thursday, until Tuesday.

Bless you

Yr: C

95. *Sunday 29 July 1917, Guy's Hospital*

Sweetheart: Just as well you didn't journey up yesterday – as I got a bit of a temp: and was rather mouldy – cheer up, I will know on Tuesday evening whether I can come down to you the next day, and will wire before starting. Patience, my chick, we will see each other on Wednesday.

Hug the chicks: Keep you safe and well

Yr: C

96. *Saturday 11 August 1917, HMS Calliope*

Sweetheart. All is well so far: I got on board at 5 o/c this morning, had some cocoa and went to sleep in front of the fire: now I am off to the flagship. Quite a good journey and lots of grub – Keep you safe and well. Here is the Mouse's picture, opened at 3 a.m. at Edinburgh!

Yr: C

97. *Sunday 12 August 1917, HMS Calliope*

Sweetheart: Since coming back from *Queen Elizabeth* yesterday, after my talk with Osmond Brock and Tommy Brand – and – not too good a night – I have practically made up my mind to go. Rather a pill, but I recognise I am not fit – and my self-respect stands in the way. Otherwise, my child, all is peace – I have oiled out of a turn of patrol, to the huge delight of all on board! Went round the ship this morning: a lot of work still to be done – I have written Holmes à Court and Spit Boyle – at Osborne, about the small son – Hope you found them all in a good skin, and tomorrow you go in to get his kit. Heart up, my chick. Bless you.

Yr: *C*

98. *Monday 13 August 1917, HMS Calliope*

Sweetheart: The pill is down: I won't say it didn't take some swallowing! I found, on seeing David Beatty, that Tripp had written to him about me, saying that I wanted a long spell off. D.B. was extremely kind: I am to write and tell him when I am fit for service once more, and he strongly advised me not to take a shore job -- My resignation has gone in, and Admiralty will be wired to today – Meanwhile I am very busy settling up ship and squadron matters. I shall probably be relieved 'bout Thursday, and then have to report to Admiralty.

Heart up, my Treasure: I am very down on my luck, but try to be philosophical.

Hug the chicks

Yr: *C*

99. *Tuesday 14 August 1917, HMS Calliope*

Sweetheart. I have your letter of Sunday: so cheered my wire got to you. We have been on a very short string this last 48 hours, so much so, that I have been sleeping in my sea-kit. News as to my successor should filter thro' today. Meanwhile I have leisure to work thro' the mountains of paper-work necessary on giving up. Dear old Tate: he went all the way to Guy's to see me – found I had decamped – and was only able to discover they were VERY doubtful as to whether I should last!

Hug the chicks: Keep your pecker up. Yr: *C*

100. *Wednesday 15 August 1917, HMS Calliope*

Sweetheart. My successor is appointed: a very old friend,[1] in command of a big ship here: I imagine he will be relieving me tomorrow (Thursday). I will wire you before leaving to go South. Programme is rather hard to settle – Club, for a tub, then Admiralty – First Lord and First Sea Lord: Medical Department: hospital or Sick Leave – probably both! – Meanwhile I have been able to get well square with the paperwork, and can give up with a clear conscience --- What a lot of rubbish one collects in two years, even under War conditions! – Heart up, my Pretty: hug the chicks – and keep a stout and stiff upper lip. I am much heartened by my interview with D.B.

Yr: C

1. Captain Rudolph Bentinck.

101. *Thursday 16 August 1917, HMS Calliope, c/o GPO*

Sweetheart: I have yr: wire: 'better things in store'. We are still on a very short string – since Monday, now, – and no word from my successor. Eh! I wish we could go out as a whole! – and have a meeting – as a finale! –

Bless you. Hug 'em all – Yr: C

102. *Saturday 18 August 1917, Caledonian United Service Club, Edinburgh*

Sweetheart. The tooth is out, and I have my sleeper booked in the St. Pancras train tonight – D.B. advised Sick Leave: said I looked better – and: 'Let me know when you are ready: there may not be a cruiser squadron, but there will be a battleship' – On the same weighing machine in this building – and in the same kit as on 2/3 July, I have gone up $1\frac{1}{2}$ lbs: – which is not so bad – considering how much I lost at Guy's.

The (Boxing) Cup came just in time for me to take it over – on my way down harbour. Had a letter from Polger a' Court saying he would keep an eye on the small son.

Bless you always. Hug the chicks. Yr: C

103. *25 September 1917, Guy's Hospital*

Sweetheart – The Kaiser's Intelligence Dept is kept well up to date? – I came in at 5 o/c[1] – and soon after eight we had the 'planes over us! However, what bombs were dropped, were more to the westward: rumour, early this morning, said Haymarket and Oxford Street – The energetic, who looked out of the window, declared they could make out the lights carried by the Hun machines.

Send you safe thro' your lunch today! Bless you always

Yr: C

1. C.E. Le Mesurier had returned from the south coast, where he had seen his son set off for The Royal Naval College, Osborne, Isle of Wight, on that day.

104. *25 September 1917, Guy's Hospital*

Sweetheart. More banging last night – a bit nearer home this time – as many casualties were taken in during the night – Tripp had a quite long talk over me, yesterday, but no operation just yet. Beast of a night – 'wough – wough' for ever so long. How are you all? And did Lou and Agnes come to blows? They tell me Hotham has taken Dick Webb's place at the Admiralty – also that Admiral Heath has gone there: pretty lucky – I think things are a bit better with me now, tho' alack, the weight has gone down.

Bless you

Yr: C

105. *Thursday 26? 27? September 1917, Guy's Hospital*

Sweetheart. I am *so* sorry: I find my yesterday's letter didn't get posted: was in bed all day and fear me you must have been uneasy. I am up now, for an hour. I say, those *Times* letters are calculated to make one think? One of the letters you sent me on was from a young A.B. who was laid out on 31/May last year: he writes to say he has been invalided out. Godfrey Munby gone!

They stoke me, little and often – once an hour. Much better night – last night – and the swallow is *really* better. Bless you always.

Yr: C

106. *Saturday 29 September 1917, Guy's Hospital*

Sweetheart. Yesterday was a day of '*riposo*', with the cubicle oak very much sported. I lay and listened, with much amusement, to a lady next door, visiting her husband, an old dug-out Naval Officer, who was a Lieutenant when I was a very junior mid: In a strong American accent, she first lectured him on the merits and demerits of a packet of sanitary paper she had brought him! And then switched on to violent abuse of her mother-in-law! His mother! A queer world – Air raids are still with us: the local world goes to ground in the Tubes about 7 o/c – and emerges towards midnight. Ninety Bernard an Admiral: we are getting on – Very little news this morning: I look forward to the small son's first bulletin about his new life.

Bless you: Hug the chicks

Yr: *C*

107. *Sunday 30 September 1917, Guy's Hospital*

Sweetheart. Recognise the paper? A relic of days with old Cotton Wool. Had a great bombardment last night: four bombs on South side of the river between here and Westminster: they say one on Waterloo. Very few casualties - I see Crawford has left *Calliope* – but they might have given him a good Dockyard appointment.

30/Sept: we are getting on thro' the year.

Bless you. Hug the chicks

Yr: *C*

108. *1 October 1917, Guy's Hospital*

Sweetheart. Many wishes for the month! Omens are good: much better nights – once the guns stop barking: much less sickness – and swallowing improving. Meantime I am kept in bed and started massage to the legs today –

Take care of yourself – Hug the chicks –

Yr: *C*

PRIME MINISTER. 'YOU YOUNG RASCAL! I NEVER SAID THAT.' NEWSBOY. 'WELL, I'LL LAY YER MEANT IT.' (Cartoon by F.H.Townsend from *Punch*, October 10, 1917)

109. *2 October 1917, Guy's Hospital*

Sweetheart. Herewith the small son's letter and his pass – He needn't be in such a tearing hurry to have his leave-ticket made out! We will sign it, on investigation, when we have been to see him? Tripp has been, but cleared out early, not to get held up by the accustomed 'Take cover' – I am to carry on, as before – and that's about all – Reggie Hall[1] said to be in good form.

My dear, I foresee my temporary appointment to the I.D.! The bombs last night were more S.W.: Army & Navy Stores? – Nuisance the boy having picked up a cold so soon.

Heart up: Hug the chicks.

Yr: *C*

THE LETTER AND THE SPIRIT.

Prime Minister. "YOU YOUNG RASCAL! I NEVER SAID THAT."
Newsboy. "WELL, I'LL LAY YER MEANT IT."

1. Captain Reginald 'Blinker' Hall, Director of Naval Intelligence.

110. *3 October 1917, Guy's Hospital*

Sweetheart. Here is a letter from old Russell – which I have answered. Tripp has been in again today, but no immediate developments to come. Given the swallow would only improve, we should simply fizz along. What an unholy mess they are making of things in Ireland! Regular jam to Sinn Fein, this brigand dying on hunger strike! Hadn't even the stamina of a Suffragette! No Service gup: I want to see more Admirals go! Bobby Benson gets a G.S.P. [Good Service Pension] – more than he deserves – Heart up, my chick. Hug the chicks.

Bless you
Yr: *C*

111. *Thursday 4 October 1917, Guy's Hospital*

Sweetheart. I have yr: letters and the Mouse's: please thank her. Also a parcel has come, so I am well off – My dear, my dear, wait for the Air Raid season to be off: 'Bout the middle of next week – but arrange to sleep at the Halls. I don't think, my child there is an earthly chance of my being ready for sea next month – so it will have to be a temp: job at Admiralty. Beast of a night last night: my cramp kept me awake in spite of dopes – However, I have slept most of today. Bring me a cake of bath soap next week? I have a few shillings left – enough to get my papers. Keep you safe and well, always.

Bless you

Yr: C

112. *Friday 5 October 1917, Guy's Hospital*

Sweetheart. Yrs: of yesterday just brought me – You ask how I am? I'm d –d if I know! And that's honest. Seems to me I'm BACK a bit – *Tanto*, I feel all right if groggy on the pins – but I fear me no chance of being found fit for sea in six weeks time: not an earthly.

No, don't go housing tame cousins: you might ask if that X ray billet is still on? Freddy Hamilton? Old Cotton Wool will chuckle: they have been great rivals all the way up the Service, and Freddy Hamilton always managed to weather him. Tommy Thorpe has to go – so I suppose Jerry Phillpotts is an Admiral – No news to give you. Nearly 1 year now – twelve long months – that it has been slops – and SECURITY! – Cheer up, my chick: we shall round the corner all right.

Hug the chicks –

Yr: C

113. *Saturday 6 October 1917, Guy's Hospital*

Sweetheart. Yrs of yesterday – Right-oh! Thursday – and put up with the Halls – for reasons of State – I want a book of stamps – *Pendennis* and the *Newcomes* and will give you back the two Thackerays I brought in with me – Otherwise nothing: a very good night again. Wonder who gets Rosyth: Look up the Navy List: scratch out Tommy Thorpe, and the man below him, and tell me who is the Senior Captain?

Little by little Haig is pushing the Huns off their remaining bit of high ground: wish we could help! – Poor old *Drake*: She has been asking for it for over a year: Ex: Halifax with Canadian convoy: drop 'em off S.W.Ireland – turning 'em over to the sea-plane and destroyer escort – and off herself to Liverpool to coal and give leave – a regular run.

Heart up, my chick: Beastly grind but will straighten out. Look after yourself.

Yr: *C*

114. *Sunday 7 October 1917, Guy's Hospital*

Sweetheart. 'A Sunday well spent means a week of content'. What is a Sunday in bed? The Sister-in-charge has determined on a Spring clean – so the Halt and the Maimed have been sent on long week-end leave – while we crocks are to shift our beds. I am up, in front of the main cooking fire as the sitting room has been bought up by visiting wives. News? Nothing in the *Observer* – Garvin is windy and wordy as ever. Curious how you find a sub-current of pro-Winston running thro' his editorials – I shall get the Naval gossip out of you – when you have seen Reggie (Hall) – wonder who relieved Heath in the III B.S.: not much of a command now, but still employment afloat.

What does the small son say this week? No more colds, I hope – and who gets Rosyth – Bit of a jar – when a C-in-C dies in the saddle: Curzon Howe? Fellowes – C.-in-C. Channel Fleet many years ago. Tryon – old George Warrender *had* been relieved? That shocking old bore next door to me will be out this week – My Heavens! Send I am not as prosy at his age! Other Naval men come and go: one is Engineer of *Cassandra* – now repairing. Interesting man, he was right thro' the War in charge of *Arethusa* – until she was finally mined. We condemned Chatham Dockyard men in chorus yesterday. Night-night, my child. Heart up.

Yr: *C*

115. *Tuesday 9 October 1917, Guy's Hospital*

Sweetheart. All sorts of letters, books and excitements these two days! George Gretton, Colin Maclean, both Macrories and Mrs Reggie Hall, dear woman.

Please send P.O. 5/- to Secretary R.U.S. Institute, Whitehall S.W.1. 'Captain LE MESURIER, subs: to Lending Library'. I think it's a bit steep: I have belonged to that mausoleum of fossils since 1902 – and paid in 'bout twenty quid in subscriptions, and for borrowing *Consulat et Empire* they rook me!

A letter from an invalided young *Calliope*: says he is now a sorter in the G.P.O. in Colchester: hope his leg will stand it – got his thigh smashed that Wednesday evening – I must get back to bed so night-night – Hug the chicks, bless 'em: Keep your pecker up –

Yr: C

116. *Wednesday/no Tuesday 23 October 1917, Guy's Hospital*

Sweetheart – A linelet. Things much about the same – Swallow going strong – good night – last night.

Bless you
Yr: C

C.E. Le Mesurier died on 10 November, 1917 and is buried at
Warblington, Hants.

Recollections of Captain E.K. Le Mesurier RN

27 November, 1978

These recollections written by 'the small son' are now in the
Liddle Collection (1914–1918), Brotherton Library, University of Leeds

Dear Mr Liddle,

. . . I have now dug up the enclosed letters from my father, written to me in June, August and September 1916, which have a bearing on Jutland.

Biographical note: The 'Lem' – 'good chap' referred to in one of my father's letters was my oldest first cousin – oldest son of my father's older brother. Havilland Le M was known to us as 'Lem'; he was wounded in France, came back to recover and went out again and was killed second time round. His younger brother was 'missing presumed dead' in Mesopotamia.

As to recollections of Osborne in 1917, my memory is pretty sketchy, I am afraid. I well remember going off for the first time (September 25, 1917) in a Dockyard Tug from South Railway Jetty at Portsmouth – my father, who had had to give up his command and was very ill indeed, came to see me go, and that was the last time I saw him, as he died in November 1917 during my first term.

We did not have serving officers as 'Term Officers' but had two civilian masters – one was A.P. Boissier who afterwards went to Harrow and the other one, M.A. Lewis, was affectionately known as 'The Bull'. I think the education was such as one would have had at a public school, except that there were no 'Classics' – see later. Facilities for games and recreation were extremely good: I remember the old rigged mast (with a safety net) on the parade ground, and having to learn to nip up and down the rigging. We played rugby only, cricket, tennis and I seem to remember there were fives courts. I know that there was an institution called 'The Log', at which each of us had to account for our activities in the 'spare time' in the afternoon; the cadet captain of one's dormitory called us by name, and we had to say 'Rugger, roller skating, gym, fives' or whatever: some people tried to account for so many activities that none could have been seriously pursued. I suppose the idea was that 'Satan finds some mischief . . .' The food was good and plentiful, and manna from Heaven to growing hungry boys. I remember taking part (I was supposed to be able to sing) in some concert show organised by Boissier: we had, among other things, to dress as Pierrots and sing some popular song of the time, but I cannot remember what it was.

We did quite a lot of Engineering instruction, including practical work which I chiefly remember as having to strip and file about ¼ inch off a steel block, which was apt to be painful till you learned not to hit your fingers: and of course boat pulling, and a bit of sailing, when the tide served, as there was little or no water at low tide. Dartmouth was, of course, much better in that respect; we did quite a lot of Engineering there too. I mention this because the 'Fisher Scheme' for officer training was, I think, in being, the object being, very sensibly, to ensure that 'Seaman' officers knew something about the engines which drove their ships. Before the 1st War there was a ridiculous, and damaging 'class conscious' rift between the Executive (Seaman) officers and the Engineers, Paymasters and Doctors, and the Fisher scheme was intended to train officers to be, partly at any rate, interchangeable between specialisations.

I list below the subjects of instruction from my Preparatory School reports (1911–17) and R.N.C. Osborne 1917–18. The reports from Dartmouth do not give individual subjects.

Prep School: Latin, French, History, Geography, Scripture, Mathematics (Geometry, Algebra, Arithmetic). Reading, Writing, Spelling, Music, Drawing.

(*Note.* Headmasters' Remarks can be quite devastating. How about this – 'I would be more satisfied if he was less self-satisfied'. I must have been a smug little brute. This is the 'Frederick' mentioned in my father's letters).

R.N.C. Osborne: Mathematics, French, Physics, History, English, Geography, Engineering, Seamanship.

I think that Dartmouth was much the same as Osborne: the education was clearly directed to the special requirements of Naval service. I do remember, also, that games and physical fitness were very important at Dartmouth; you were thought a bit odd if you liked, say, birdwatching or photography!

The education system certainly produced a 'very good standard article' for what was required by the R.N.: but, looking back, it left great gaps in appreciation of the arts – e.g. music or pictures – which I have had to develop later on. – I do not say that one could *not* work on the arts – but it was not usual.

I, for example, enjoyed games, was adequate at most though nowhere near the top class, – and therefore slotted easily into the usual pattern.

Incidentally, I also have my father's certificates, and I see that in his certificate for the rank of Lieutenant at the Royal Naval College (Greenwich I presume) dated October 1889, the subjects of examination are Algebra 28/100, Geometry 54/100, Dynamics 49/100, Statics and Hydrostatics 47/100, Physics 34/100, Steam Engine 59/100, French 178/200, Winds and Currents 87/100, Practical Navigation 172/200 Nautical Astronomy 122/200, Nautical Surveying 61/100, Instruments 27/40, Observations 57/60 and Extra Paper (whatever that was) 56/200.

Papa got a 3rd class at the R.N.C. but in November 1889 he got 1sts in Gunnery and Torpedo. His Torpedo Exam was marked as papers on Electricity & Torpedoes and Whitehead, and Practical on the launch, also a

Viva Voce mark; for Gunnery he had 'Heavy and Light Gun, Field Exercise, Ammunition, Theoretical and practical use of the Director, Field & Machine Gun & Battery, Turret and Cutlass & Pistol (this had HP's of 30 ex bow). In his examination for rating up from Naval Cadet to midshipman (1884) refers almost entirely to navigation, & handling of boats, rigging, etc but the last item is 'Knowledge of the Great Gun, Rifle, Pistol & Cutlass exercises'.

None of this is really relevant to the information on W.W.I which you seek: but in the course of digging up what I could find for you, I became interested in the 'training requirement' for a young officer e.g. my father at the end of the last century, as compared with that for a young officer (cadet 1917–21, midshipman 1922–24, lieutenant 1924–25) i.e.myself. It was fairly widely held, I think, that the usual 'Seaman' officer prior to W.W.I, while very good at his seamanship job, was impervious to any ideas on the technical side of his profession: but it would seem that even back in the late 1880s they were beginning to have to learn the language of the technical revolution that was to come, even if the extent of teaching was limited.

I have 'gone on' on this subject rather too much, I fear: but I am and always have been interested in the question of the proper balance between 'technical' and 'command' experience and its effect on promotion prospects. The 'command' side was, naturally I suppose, the main ladder to promotion beyond Captain, and so it happened that my own career tended to be mainly on the technical (gunnery) side, partly in the pre-W.W.II years after I qualified in Gunnery in 1930, when we were working up to the war: when, after the war I managed to get out of the technical run of jobs, opportunities for getting sea-going command were very limited indeed. However, that is all old history now: but the Navy did not, in the pre-war years, recruit nearly enough trained scientists and 'design-engineers' or 'development- engineers' at any rate in the weapons field, and as a result, specialised executive branch officers like myself had to fill the gaps. We learnt to work happily with – and appreciate the point of view of, and the method of working of – the scientists and technicians; it has surprised me, looking back, how I've managed not to make any really bad errors in spite of being only partly technical and since it fell to us, often enough, to make the final decision as to what was, and what was not, feasible.

Thank you for your kind words at the end of your letter. I happen to feel that a long history of service to one's country is something of which to be proud – but have the uncomfortable feeling that to say so nowadays causes many people to fall about laughing! – I suppose that the collapse of the Commonwealth which we ran with considerable success, has much to do with it: the opportunity for a certain type of man to exercise his skill in more or less disinterested, and devoted, service (whether overseas Government Service or the 'fighting' service or whatever) has largely disappeared: and it is a great pity that the 'emergent nations' have not been able to tap that source to help them 'emerge', though I suppose it is natural for them to feel that – having at last got their long trousers on – they must do it all their own way!

Maybe I am wrong – my son-in-law who is in a Foreign Office post in Dubai at present, has told me that 'Brits' are popular in the Gulf States as they work hard, give good service, and don't cost nearly as much as Americans – So perhaps I am too pessimistic.

I apologise for this rambling screed – let me know if I can do anything else.

Yours sincerely

Le Mesurier

Postcard from Valletta, Malta, sent by their father to
B. & J. (Benjamin and Julia)

This is *Belfast* going into Malta. Can you see one figure on the front of the bridge standing up higher than the rest? That's me.

HMS *Belfast* was the largest size of cruiser in World War II. She had seven decks and a complement of over 800 men. Her keel was laid down on 10 December, 1936 at Harland & Wolff Limited, Belfast, and she was launched on St Patrick's Day 1938 by Mrs Neville Chamberlain, wife of the Prime Minister. *Belfast* displaced 11,500 tons, but this figure increased when she was repaired after being mined in 1940.

Time Line of the Great War

1914

Jun 28	Archduke Franz Ferdinand assassinated at Sarajevo.
Jul 28	Austria Hungary declares war on Serbia.
Aug 1–3	Germany declares war against Russia and France.
Aug 4	Germany invades Belgium. Britain declares war on Germany.
Aug 16	British Expeditionary Force (BEF) starts landing in France (escorted by Navy) and joins French and Belgian troops at Mons.
Aug 20	Germans occupy Brussels.
Aug 30	British naval victory in Heligoland Bight.
Aug 30	Two Russian armies defeated at Tannenburg, N. Germany.
Sept 5–12	Battle of the Marne. Allies drive enemy from Paris.
Oct 30	First Battle of Ypres.
Nov 5	Britain declares war on Turkey.
Dec 8	Battle of the Falkland Islands. British naval victory

1915

Jan 22	Battle of the Dogger Bank. British naval victory
Feb 17	Germans start sea blockade of Britain.
Mar 1	Allied fleets start sea blockade of Germany.
Mar 4	HMS *Queen Elizabeth* bombards the Dardanelles.
Mar 18	HMS *Ocean* and HMS *Irresistible* sunk by mines off Dardanelles.
Apr 5	King George V banishes alcohol from Royal Table.
Apr 23	First German gas attacks drive Allies back from Ypres.
Apr 24	Anzacs land in the Dardanelles.
May 23	Italy declares war on Austria.
Aug 4	Fall of Warsaw.
Aug 15	National Register (population census) is taken in Britain.
Sept 25–28	Battle of Loos. British victory on Western Front.
Dec 7	Turks trap British army at Kut in Mesopotamia. Oil supplies for Navy are threatened.
Dec 19	Navy begins evacuating troops from Gallipoli and the Dardanelles.

1916

Jan 27	First Military Service Bill passed.
Feb 21	Germany attacks at Verdun.
Mar 4	German mine-layer *Moewe* reported reaching Germany after sinking 50,000 tons of shipping.
Apr 19	Irish rebellion in Dublin. Arrest of Sir Roger Casement.
Apr 29	Anglo-Indian garrison surrenders at Kut in Mesopotamia.
May 9	Daylight Saving Act passed by Parliament.
May 11	Ireland: Easter Rising casualties: 794 civilians, 521 police and troops.
May 25	First Air Board established in Britain.

May 31	Battle of Jutland. Navy suffers losses but retains command of North Sea. German High Seas Fleet retreats to harbour and stays there.
Jun 4	Russia opens Brusilov offensive, smashing Austrian Front Line.
Jun 5	Lord Kitchener drowns off Orkney when HMS *Hampshire* is mined on her way to Russia for a military and diplomatic mission.
Jun 21	Allies demand that Greece demobilses.
July 1	British offensive on The Somme. 19,000 British casualties on first day.
Jul–Nov	Half a million Allied lives lost on The Somme front, defending Paris.
Jul 8	German submarine *Deutschland* reaches New York.
Aug 2	Sir Roger Casement, Irish Home Rule leader, is hanged in London.
Aug 18–19	German Admiral Scheer ventures into N. Sea and sinks two light cruisers – *Falmouth* and *Nottingham*; Navy damages *Westfalen*
Sept 15	First use of tanks on Western Front.
Sept 26	Allies capture Combles and Thiépval.
Dec 7	Lloyd George Prime Minister after fall of Asquith Government.
Dec 11	War Cabinet established.

1917

Jan 1	America declares 1916 most prosperous year in its history.
Feb 1	Germany begins 'unrestricted' submarine warfare.
Feb 3	America severs diplomatic links with Germany.
Mar 9	British capture Baghdad.
Mar 15	Emperor of Russia abdicates.
Apr 5	America declares war on Germany.
Apr 9	Battle of Arras begins on Western Front.
Apr 16	Food riots in Berlin.
May 2	King George V asks his subjects to eat a quarter less bread.
May 3	Mutiny in sections of French Army.
Jun 1	British Convoy System is formed to protect merchant shipping.
Jun 19	King George V orders Royals to drop German titles in favour of Windsor.
Jul 31	Battle of Passchendaele. Allies attack near Ypres.
Aug 11	Russian P.M. (Kerensky) pledges continuing support for Allies.
Oct 6-7	Russian ('October') Revolution. Lenin's Bolsheviks come to power.
Nov 20	Battle of Cambrai (Western Front) sees use of armoured vehicles/tanks.

1918

Jan 9	President Wilson's 'Fourteen Points', outlining war aims.
Jan 22–23	First meeting of Allied Naval Council.
Mar 3	Treaty of Brest Litovsk takes Russia out of the war.
Apr 23	Navy bottles up German submarine bases in Zeebrugge and Ostend.

Jun 19	British Government introduces general rationing.
Jun 26	German gun 'Big Bertha' shells Paris from a range of 65 miles.
Jul 15	Second Battle of the Marne. Germany's last offensive halted.
Aug 29	Allies win victory at Amiens.
Oct	Lawrence of Arabia leads Arabs into Damascus.
Oct 7	Germany seeks an armistice, followed by Austria Hungary on 26 October 1917.
Nov 7	Mutiny and riots in German ports.
Nov 9	German Kaiser abdicates and Crown Prince renounces succession.
Nov 11	Germany signs Armistice.
Nov 21	German High Seas Fleet surrenders and is impounded at Scapa Flow.

1919

Jun 21	German sailors scuttle High Seas Fleet in Scapa Flow.

Books and other sources used

Bennett, Geoffrey, *The Battle of Jutland*, Wordsworth Editions Ltd, 1999

Bryant, Mark, and Simon Heneage, *Dictionary of British Cartoonists and Caricaturists 1730–1980*, Scolar Press, 1994

Conway's *All the World's Fighting Ships*, 1906–21, Conway Maritime Press, 1985

Corbett, Sir Julian S., *History of the Great War. Naval Operations Vol III*, Imperial War Museum and The Battery Press, 1928

Encyclopedia Britannica Vol 29, 13th edition, London and New York, pp 617–28

Gordon, Andrew, *The Rules of the Game: Jutland and British Naval Command*, John Murray, 1996

Grove, Eric, *Big Fleet Actions*, Brockhampton Press, 1991

Harper, J.E.T., *The Truth About Jutland*, John Murray, 1927

Hewison, W.S., *This Great Harbour Scapa Flow*, Orkney Press, 1985

Marder, Arthur J., *From the Dreadnought to Scapa Flow: Vol I, The Road to War 1904–14*, Oxford University Press, 1961

Marder, Arthur J., *From the Dreadnought to Scapa Flow: Vol II, The War Years: to the Eve of Jutland*, Oxford University Press, 1965

Mercer, Derrick, ed. *Chronicle of the 20th Century*, Chronicle Communications, Longman, 1988

Punch Vol CLII January–June 1917, Whitefriars, London

Punch Vol CLIII July–December 1917, Whitefriars, London

Tarrant, V.E., *Jutland, The German Perspective*, Arms and Armour Press, 1995

Thompson, Julian, *The Imperial War Museum Book of The War at Sea 1914–18*, Sidgwick & Jackson in association with the Imperial War Museum, 2005.

The Times newspaper, Friday 7 July, 1916, *Admiral Jellicoe's Despatch with Sir David Beatty's Report* (pp 17, 19 and 21)

Acknowledgements

My thanks go first to Roderick Suddaby, Keeper of the Imperial War Museum's Department of Documents, where my grandfather's original 1916–17 letters are held under reference 65/103/1–2. Without his informed opinion that these Letters are 'a significant historical source' and his help with transcription and interpretation, this book would not have happened.

Heartfelt thanks are due to Major General Julian Thompson, CB, OBE, for validating that opinion by including extracts in his book *The Imperial War Museum Book of the War at Sea 1914–18*, and most especially for writing the Foreword. I am also indebted to the National Archive and the staff of *The Naval Review*, in particular Rear Admiral J.R. Hill, RN, and Commander Alastair Wilson, RN, for their unstinting help in identifying contemporary photographs and personnel and helping to keep me on track. However, any mistakes in fact or interpretation I must acknowledge as my own. Readers' comments, criticisms and added information will be most welcome.

Among the many helpful 'picture' personnel are Michael Moody and David Bell of the Imperial War Museum's Art Department and Photographic Archive respectively, David Mackie of the Orkney Library & Archive and Andrew Cheung, Curator of Plans and Photos, Historic Photographs and Ship Plans Section of the National Maritime Museum, Greenwich. My cousins, Lieutenant Colonel Benjamin Le Mesurier, Ewa-Christina Le Mesurier and Mrs Julia Gowlland (née Le Mesurier) have shared their knowledge of family history, provided photographs and given copyright permission for Captain E.K. Le Mesurier's *Recollections*. Mrs Helen Newman, niece of Charles Le Mesurier's niece, Nell Inman, also spurred me on with family archive material.

Mrs Liz Carter, widow of my late brother Commander C.D. Carter, RN (formerly Superintendent of Rosyth Dockyard) was invaluable in taking me to Orkney to visit the Lyness Museum, Melsetter House, and the staff of *The Orcadian* newspaper in Kirkwall. Her daughter, Alison Downie and son-in-law Alan Downie have also contributed. Alan led me to John Ferguson of Radio Orkney who recommended W.S. Hewison's useful book *This Great Harbour, Scapa Flow* (published by The Orkney Press).

Thanks go to my young computer wizard, Dan Cutts, and to Angela Blair and Larissa Brisbane for other technical assistance. Carol Carl-Sime cast a 'fresh eye' over the galley proofs. Clare Everett-Allen of the Brotherton Library at Leeds University and the staff at King's College London's Archives and Corporate Records Services helped chase manuscripts.

I am especially grateful to my publisher, Jane Drake of Wessex Books, her assistant Bev Barton, and former publisher-colleague Douglas Stuckey for their expertise, knowledge and support. Lastly, huge thanks must go to my husband, Emeritus Professor Fred Bachrach CBE, whose faith in this project has never wavered.

H.B.